TRADITION. EXPERIENCE.
TRANSFORMATION.

Formatio books from InterVarsity Press follow the rich tradition of the church in the journey of spiritual formation. These books are not merely about being informed, but about being transformed by Christ and conformed to his image. Formatio stands in InterVarsity Press's evangelical publishing tradition by integrating God's Word with spiritual practice and by prompting readers to move from inward change to outward witness. InterVarsity Press uses the chambered nautilus for Formatio, a symbol of spiritual formation because of its continual spiral journey outward as it moves from its center. We believe that each of us is made with a deep desire to be in God's presence. Formatio books help us to fulfill our deepest desires and to become our true selves in light of God's grace.

LYNNE M. BAAB

FASTING

Spiritual Freedom
Beyond Our Appetites

IVP Books

An imprint of InterVarsity Press
Downers Grove, Illinois

InterVarsity Press
P.O. Box 1400, Downers Grove, IL 60515-1426
World Wide Web: www.ivpress.com
E-mail: mail@ivpress.com

InterVarsity Press® is the book-publishing division of InterVarsity Christian Fellowship/USA®, a student movement active on campus at hundreds of universities, colleges and schools of nursing in the United States of America, and a member movement of the International Fellowship of Evangelical Students. For information about local and regional activities, write Public Relations Dept., InterVarsity Christian Fellowship/USA, 6400 Schroeder Rd., P.O. Box 7895, Madison, WI 53707-7895, or visit the IVCF website at <www.intervarsity.org>.

Scripture quotations, unless otherwise noted, are from the New Revised Standard Version of the Bible, copyright 1989 by the Division of Christian Education of the National Council of the Churches of Christ in the USA. Used by permission. All rights reserved.

The information provided in this book is intended to describe the potential benefits of many forms of fasting, including fasting from all food. If you have any kind of medical condition, including an eating disorder, or if you take any medication prescribed by a physician, the decision to engage in fasting from all food should be made only after consulting with a physician. Nothing in this book should be used as a substitute for professional medical care or treatment.

All personal fasting stories are used with permission. All names and some identifying details have been changed.

Design: Cindy Kiple
Images: Doable/Getty Images

ISBN-10: 0-8308-3501-6
ISBN-13: 978-0-8308-3501-0

Printed in the United States of America ∞

Library of Congress Cataloging-in-Publication Data

Baab, Lynne M.
    Fasting: spiritual freedom beyond our appetites/Lynne Baab.
        p. cm
    Includes bibliographical references and index.
    ISBN-13: 978-0-8308-3501-0 (pbk.: alk. paper)
    ISBN-10: 0-8308-3501-6 (pbk.: alk. paper)
    1. Fasting—Religious aspects—Christianity. I. Title.

BV5055.B33 2006
248.4'7—dc22

                                                                    2006030479

P	18	17	16	15	14	13	12	11	10	9	8	7	6	5	4	3	2	1
Y	21	20	19	18	17	16	15	14	13	12	11	10	09	08	07	06		

CONTENTS

Acknowledgments

I couldn't have written this book without the many people who told me their fasting stories. Equally valuable are the many other people who told me why they don't fast, why they quit fasting or what they wish they knew about fasting. Thank you, all of you, for honoring me with your confidences. This book wouldn't exist without you.

I am also extremely grateful for the people who let me think out loud with them as I was processing issues about fasting. They made significant suggestions, many of which are incorporated into the text of the book. A warm thank you to Julie Christensen, Ann Kelley, Rev. Steve Lympus, Rev. Dave Shull, Tara Taylor, Rev. Lynne Faris Blessing, Rev. Ellen Schulz and Rev. Reneé Sundberg.

Dan Johnson researched four passages on fasting in several new translations of the Bible. Rev. Dale Youngs gave me notes from several sermons. Scotty Kessler sent me extensive notes on fasting in the Bible. Garth Warren sent me a diary of a two-week fast. I am so grateful to each of you for your help.

I also want to thank Marian Neuhouser, Ph.D., who helped me with medical questions, and Kara Bazzi and Rev. Dave Rohrer, who helped me with implications for people with eating disorders. Any mistakes are my responsibility, not theirs.

Several people read the manuscript and made many helpful suggestions. An enthusiastic thank-you to Anne Baumgartner, Rev. Lynne Faris Blessing, Joleen Burgess, Rev. Monica Elvig, Kimberlee Conway Ireton, Lisa Jeremiah, Rev. Steve Lympus and Susan Forshey. To all of you, I can't thank you enough for your help as well as your friendship.

My InterVarsity Press editor for this book and *Sabbath Keeping*, Dave Zimmerman, has been terrific. Thank you, Dave, for the many practical ways you give me support and guidance as a writer and help make my books better.

My wonderful and supportive husband, Dave Baab, fits into most of the categories above. He told me his fasting stories, and he read my manuscript. I am particularly grateful for the countless times he sat at the dinner table and allowed me to think out loud about one issue or another related to this book. For me, those moments went by quickly, but I imagine that for him, it seemed I was talking a very long time. Thank you, Dave, for your loving, listening ear and for so much more.

1

AN INVITATION TO FREEDOM

For freedom Christ has set us free. Stand firm, therefore,
and do not submit again to a yoke of slavery.

GALATIANS 5:1

Seattle has its own smaller version of the Statue of Liberty. She gazes over Puget Sound, standing tall in a park that swarms with joggers and parents pushing strollers. From the rear she looks just like the statue in New York City, with flowing robes, a torch in her hand, and a crown with spikes.

Her face, however, is totally different. While Lady Liberty in New York has a stern and austere expression, Seattle's near replica has a soft, almost fleshy face. She looks like an indulgent grandmother.

I've always loved the "real" Statue of Liberty, including her stern expression. Standing in New York harbor as a symbol of welcome to those in need, Lady Liberty's face reminds me that freedom is costly, requiring sacrifice, discipline and commitment.

We live in a culture obsessed with freedom and liberty, but our version of liberty has become indulgent and soft, like the face on Seattle's statue. We forget that freedom comes at a price; we act as if liberty means the right to be self-absorbed and self-focused.

While we skim from one enticing and absorbing topic to another—beauty aids and sex techniques, cell phone calling plans and personal organizers, exercise shoes and kitchen remodels—we barely notice that these thoughts take the place of other concerns we value more highly. We so easily become enslaved to things that ultimately have little meaning.

Here's the rub: we inhabit a culture obsessed with liberty, but we habituate ourselves into bondage. We've forgotten what lack feels like and what liberty tastes like.

AN INVITATION

Jesus Christ has redeemed us from the power of sin and death so we can live in freedom. Jesus said to his disciples, "If the Son makes you free, you will be free indeed" (Jn 8:36). The apostle Paul echoed that wonderful truth: "The law of the Spirit of life in Christ Jesus has set you free from the law of sin and of death" (Rom 8:2). How can we experience more of that liberty in our everyday lives?

Fasting, an ancient practice, encourages us to grow in true freedom. In fasting, God invites us to experience the kind of freedom that is rooted in healthy discipline and meaningful sacrifice, the kind of freedom that reflects the awesome reality that we have been freed from sin and death. Fasting offers the opportunity to step back from our culture and cross the doorway into God's presence. Fasting ushers us into a reflective place where we can listen to God and pray wholeheartedly for things that really matter.

Christians today are embracing fasting in a variety of forms. This discipline addresses some of the challenges of trying to live faithfully in a frantic and materialistic consumer culture. Fasting today includes abstaining from food, just like Christians did centuries ago, but also from news media, entertainment, information, shopping, email and the Internet, and other aspects of daily life.

During the writing of this book, I was praying for the thousandth time about an obstacle a friend had been facing for almost two years—something that should have been resolved much more quickly. As I was praying, the idea came into my mind that perhaps we should fast together as we prayed for the problem. My friend agreed, and we set a date for a one-day fast.

Fasting is like tying a ribbon around your finger to remember God.

ANNA, A MUSICIAN
IN HER THIRTIES

I prayed about how to fast on that day. As I looked at my schedule, I found I had three consecutive appointments that would require a total of four car trips ranging from fifteen to thirty minutes each. When I drive I always play music, turned up loud.

I decided to fast from music on those four car rides, expecting that the silence would remind me to pray. So on that pleasant sunny day I set out on my first expedition with the car windows open. I noticed something surprising right away: my muffler was beginning to go out! I hadn't noticed it earlier because of the music I always play. I wondered what else I might be missing in my life because I do so many things the same way, day after day.

On the first two trips, the shorter ones, I prayed fervently for my preferred solution to my friend's problem. On the third trip, I realized I had spent no time trying to hear God's voice on the subject, so I began to ask God to teach me how to pray for the problem. I found myself thanking God for the ways he has helped my friend cope and for the ways he has brought good things to her because of this unresolved issue. Then my prayers changed again, and I began to focus on her family. By the fourth car trip, I was praying for the problem in a totally different way, and this new way of praying continued to influence my prayers after the fast day ended.

On the two longer car trips, I didn't pray continuously. My thoughts would drift off to other things. But, as I expected, the absence of music, the hum of traffic and the roar of my muffler reminded me numerous times that I had committed myself to pray while I drove.

I am free to lightheartedly stop a habit for a day and experience new things with God.

This form of fasting communicates a profound freedom. I don't have to do things the same way, day after day. I am not a slave to my habits. I can change things around, I can try new things, and I can experience companionship with God in new ways. I am free to light-heartedly stop a habit for a day and experience new things with God, even as my heart is heavy and I am praying fervently for my friend's needs.

FREEDOM, NOT SELF-PUNISHMENT

As I write about many specific issues related to fasting, I want to argue that fasting is essentially about freedom: The freedom to make time to read the Bible and draw near to God. The freedom to pray passionately for the needs of people near and far. The freedom to listen to God and change the direction of our prayers. The freedom to feel the full range of human emotions mirrored so passionately in the Psalms. The freedom to embrace a rhythm that includes days and weeks of ordinary, everyday consumption of food and entertainment, days of fasting, and great celebrations of feasting, when we eat special foods and indulge in favorite activities.

Linda, a medical assistant who was raised in a Roman Catholic family, remembers the Fridays of her childhood, when her family ate macaroni and cheese or Tuna Helper instead of meat. She reflects, "Fasting in my childhood was about self-punishment because we are sinful." She does not fast today because she doesn't believe God wants us to punish ourselves.

Linda is right that God doesn't want us to punish ourselves. Fasting as self-punishment denies the freedom God gives us in Christ. Fasting as self-punishment does not create space for prayer, give energy to our prayers or enable us to listen to God.

Jodie, an office manager in her fifties, echoes the theme of self-punishment, taking it even further. She is adamant that "not eating is not good." She cannot see any way that fasting could be a healthy spiritual discipline. Fasting, Jodie says,

> runs the risk of being theologically or spiritually abusive. It surely calls on the perceived dichotomy between body and soul, physical and spiritual, as if there can be no integration, no unity, no fullness of self. I find that worldview to be a denial of God's good creation, and one that has caused innumerable problems for Christians over the years. Deny the body. Deny the appetites. Don't have fun. Of course, the other side—indulge to excess—is equally spiritually bankrupt and self-destructive. We are a part of creation, and our bodies and appetites are a part of creation. We should rejoice in that, not deny and reject it. Our spirits are intimately connected to our bodies, and to deny the latter is to cripple the former.

Jodie is right that indulgence to excess is spiritually bankrupt and self-destructive. If we listen to our culture, encouragement to indulge to excess is all we hear. Fasting provides times to back away from excess in order to pray. In that backing away and in that praying, we often rediscover a healthier pathway for everyday life.

Fasting is not about practicing extreme self-denial day after day, year after year. Fasting lasts only for a set time. When we fast, we affirm that we are healthiest when we embrace rhythms. Sometimes we need to celebrate abundance; sometimes we need to submit ourselves to discipline.

Jodie believes that fasting denies the relationship between the body and spirit. I would say in response that if we do it well, fasting more than

> *A relationship with God is not something that happens only in our mind. It involves our total self, which is why disciplines such as fasting retrain our bodies.*

> JAN JOHNSON,
> *FASTING AND SIMPLICITY*

any other spiritual discipline affirms the integral relationship between body and soul and spirit. It helps us steer a path between unhealthy self-indulgence and excessive discipline. The key to healthy fasting is to understand the purpose of spiritual disciplines.

EVERYDAY DISCIPLINES AND SPIRITUAL DISCIPLINES

We engage in any kind of discipline because we believe our lives are shaped by the habits we engage in every day. I take out the garbage so the house doesn't smell. I balance the checkbook to make sure I have money in my account. I exercise regularly so my blood pressure and other health indicators will stay at healthy levels and so I can sleep well at night. All of us engage in countless small disciplines that make our lives work well.

We can take habits too far or not far enough. I could choose not to exercise at all. When I do that, I stop sleeping well, I gain weight and my health suffers. Or I could exercise all the time until it becomes a compulsion and I can't think of anything else. That would be equally destructive. Instead, I've tried to figure out the right amount of exercise for my body. In the same way, I could check my bank balance every day or not at all. Instead, I try to track money in a way that keeps my spending wise and under control but doesn't allow me to become obsessed.

Spiritual disciplines are similar. We have a lifetime to explore the spiritual disciplines and figure out what works best for us, what helps us draw near to Jesus and grow in faith. What works at one stage of life may not be so effective at another stage, so we need to try new things from time to time. At all stages of life, we can fall into excess very easily. We can ignore the disciplines that might help us grow in faith, or we can become obsessed with them and go too far.

Tony Jones, in his helpful book *The Sacred Way,* writes, "The goal of Christian spirituality is to be enlivened by God's Spirit." He goes on to affirm that the words *practice* and *discipline* are helpful terms to consider when discussing what Christian spirituality looks like in everyday life. Since ancient times, Christians have understood that everyday spirituality thrives because of the spiritual practices or disciplines we engage in day after day and week after week. Some of those practices are what Jones calls "contemplative," including spiritual direction, many kinds of prayer and sacred reading of Scripture. Other practices, such as fasting, engage the body directly. Jones recommends that we imagine the parallels between the Christian life and learning to play a musical instrument or working out in a committed way or improving at playing chess. Just as discipline and practice are essential in each of those endeavors, so discipline and practice are equally essential in growing close to God in Jesus Christ, allowing God's Spirit to enliven us.

As we explore the discipline of fasting, we have to remain clear that we don't engage in spiritual practices or disciplines to punish ourselves. John Piper, author of many books on desiring God, is adamant that Christian fasting rests on the finished work of the Bridegroom, Jesus, who has bought our salvation by his death. The Holy Spirit is a pledge of our inheritance (Eph 1:13-14). Jesus' love arouses in us a hunger for the fullness of God's presence in us and with us. Fasting expresses that hunger.

Christian fasting is simply not about

When I fast, the purpose is to notice the false, non-life-giving things that I'm attached to. And to purposely attempt to attach to the ways of God.

JANET, A CHURCH STAFF
MEMBER IN HER FIFTIES

self-punishment, as Linda experienced in her childhood. Jesus redeemed us; any punishment we deserve belongs in the past. Jodie observed that self-deprivation seems rooted in self-hate. When I stop en-
joyable activities in order to take out the garbage, balance the checkbook
or exercise, I'm not engaging in self-deprivation because I hate myself; I
do these small acts of discipline because I want to take care of the precious life God has given me. In the same way, I embrace fasting as a way
to affirm my desire for God's presence.

I love that amusing memory of the day I fasted from music in the car
to pray for my friend's need. The first thing I noticed was the unexpected
noise of my failing muffler. To some extent, fasting is just that simple. We
remove something habitual so we can experience something new. We
long for the fullness of God's presence, so we remove something from
our life for a season in order to get a glimpse of God, through prayer, in
a new way. Fasting gives us the freedom to do that.

Christian fasting, when it is done in a biblical and spiritually healthy
way, is not a way of avoiding life, as Jodie believes. Fasting is a way of
experiencing something new in life. Our appetites are a part of creation,
just as Jodie says. But we can discipline some of our appetites for a time
in order to embrace other appetites, particularly our desire for intimacy
with God through prayer.

A DEFINITION OF FASTING

As we come to the end of this first chapter, I want to suggest a definition
of fasting. What is fasting in the Christian life? Christian fasting is the
voluntary denial of something for a specific time, for a spiritual purpose,
by an individual, family, community or nation.

Many readers may find that, based on this broad definition, they al-
ready practice some version of fasting. Most of the religions of the world
recommend fasting. Our task in this book is to explore and develop a
distinctively Christian view of fasting. This understanding will be

grounded in the Bible and informed by Christian history.

We will look at many specific and practical ways to fast that meet the needs of our time. We will examine various aspects of the above definition, and we will explore many characteristics of Christian fasting that round out the concepts in the definition. Because fasting is becoming more common among Christians from many different traditions, we will hear voices of real people who fast in a variety of ways. Their voices will help make fasting come alive for us.

QUESTIONS FOR REFLECTION, JOURNALING AND DISCUSSION

1. When you consider the word *fasting,* what thoughts and feelings come to mind, both positive and negative?
2. Before beginning this book, what had you heard or read about fasting?
3. What questions do you have about fasting?

FOR PRAYER

Bring your longings and fears about fasting to God in prayer. Bring your questions about fasting to God. Ask God to open your heart to hear his guidance.

2

FOOD AND FASTING TODAY

Then the word of the LORD of hosts came to me:
Say to all the people of the land and the priests:
When you fasted and lamented in the fifth month and
in the seventh, for these seventy years,
was it for me that you fasted? And when you eat and when you drink,
do you not eat and drink only for yourselves?

ZECHARIAH 7:4-6

When Queen Esther prepared to approach the king of Persia to ask him to spare the Jewish people from destruction, she fasted and prayed for God's help, and she asked all the Jews in her city to fast and pray with her (Esther 4:16). When the early Christians wanted to consecrate new leaders, they fasted and prayed for them (Acts 14:23). When the Pilgrims on the Mayflower knew they were only a few days from land, they decided to spend a day fasting and praying that God would bless their new colony.

Fasting and praying occur together frequently throughout the Bible. Christians throughout history have fasted when they prayed for intense needs and when they wanted to free up money to give to the poor. In many churches in Africa, Asia, and Central and South America, fasting is an everyday part of congregational life, with weekly fast days as well as longer fasts at certain times of the year.

Yet for many Christians in the United States and other Western countries, fasting is an alien and distasteful practice, often associated with excessive self-discipline and self-punishment. How did we get to this place? How can fasting be viewed as a natural, healthy and spiritually rich practice in some parts of the world while being viewed as unnatural and unhealthy in other places?

Several factors have brought us to the point where fasting is so misunderstood. First, as we saw in chapter one, our culture tells us that every desire should be fulfilled as soon as possible. The consumer economy of the industrialized world requires, by definition, that people consume. At every turn we are encouraged to purchase food, cars, clothes, furniture, knickknacks, electronic devices, toys and so forth. We are also urged to purchase experiences, the latest forms of recreation and pleasure. Without a constant stream of people purchasing things, the economy would flounder.

As a result of the barrage of advertising we have experienced all our lives, we have become fearful of deprivation of any kind. We have become subtly convinced that the indulgence of every appetite is psychologically and physically healthy. *If I forego any pleasures, I might be diminished as a per-*

> **Fasting in American and other prosperous western nations is almost incomprehensible because we are brainwashed by a consumer culture. We are taught to experience the good life by consuming, not by renouncing consumption.**

JOHN PIPER,
*A HUNGER FOR GOD:
DESIRING GOD THROUGH
FASTING AND PRAYER*

son! If I skip a meal, I might starve! These voices deeply limit our ability to embrace Christian disciplines such as fasting. In several sections of this book, we will explore ways that fasting addresses our addiction to consumption.

SOME EQUATIONS

Another reason fasting fell out of favor in the twentieth century is connected to our strange relationship with food. Until recently, fasting was defined solely as abstaining from some or all foods, and the way we view food in the United States and other Western countries has become convoluted. Food now carries an emotional weight far beyond its past role as a means of nourishment and a reason for family and friends to gather.

A brief history of eating reveals connections and contradictions over the past thousand years that continue to impact us today. In the medieval period, thinness and not eating were equated with being spiritual. This equation came from the fact that some famous Christians embraced fasting in extreme forms. During the Renaissance another equation became influential: thin equaled poor. Only the rich could get enough to eat, therefore eating in abundance was equated with being prosperous. During the twentieth century, the equation changed again. People, particularly women, began to embrace dieting because thinness was equated with being beautiful.

All of these equations and contradictions, both from past centuries and the present day, have an impact on the way we view food and eating. In this chapter we will consider the place of fasting in the midst of these contradictions. Some people, because of excessive engagement with dieting, simply should never fast from food. In the first chapter we saw that fasting can be easily adapted to involve abstaining from things other than food, so everyone who desires to experience this ancient discipline can find a form of fasting that works for them.

MEN AND WOMEN IN A DIET CULTURE

Many women and some men in our time and especially in North America experience significant challenges with food. They are deeply affected by our culture's emphasis on dieting. Because the average body weight of female models and actresses has declined steadily over the past five decades, more women look overweight when compared with the media "ideal." In fact, many female models and actresses are so thin they look like they've been fasting for months. At the same time, male models and actors have become visibly more muscular, with no fat covering those muscles. All of this has resulted in a culture of dieting and obsession with food and weight.

While this culture affects both men and women, many more women are deeply influenced by it. Women are more likely than men to experience eating disorders. While the number of men with anorexia or bulimia is rising, many more women have a history of an eating disorder. This unique relationship between women and food dates back many centuries, particularly in Western countries.

In the days of the early church, consumption of specific foods was believed to be connected to sexual arousal. Because celibacy was valued, especially for women, fasting from those particular foods was recommended. Fasting in general was also recommended, particularly for women, because a significant reduction in calories reduces sexual desire.

In the middle ages, both women and men in convents and monasteries engaged in regular fasting, but some women carried it to amazing levels. Catherine of Sienna (1347-1380), who wrote widely and eloquently about the Christian faith, ate almost nothing. Several other Christian women of her time were known and admired for becoming sick around food. At least one Christian woman in the fifteenth century died of self-starvation. In the seventeenth century, Saint Veronica was known for her extreme fasts.

Joan Jacobs Brumberg, a scholar who studied the historical roots of eating disorders, observes:

> Although fasting and restrictive eating was a widely noted charac-
> teristic of medieval spirituality, it did not engage both genders in
> the same manner or to the same degree. There are few cases of male
> saints who claimed or were claimed by others to be incapable of
> eating. In the medieval period fasting was fundamental to the
> model of female holiness.

Brumberg goes on to note that in the Victorian period a kind of prud-
ishness about eating emerged among middle-class and upper-class
women. After all, a woman who ate and drank would inevitably have to
urinate and move her bowels, things that were indelicate and unmen-
tionable for women in polite society. So middle-class women in Victorian
England and the United States often ate as little as possible and were admired for it.

In most cultures around the world before 1900, being plump was associated with prosperity and good health. A moderate amount of fat was
considered to be an advantage when disease struck. However, in the
early twentieth century, thinness for women became the ideal.

As early as 1907 an article in *The Atlantic Monthly* described a
woman's agony because she had gained weight. In the 1920s the
women's clothing industry turned to ready-to-wear fashion, which required standard sizing and which allowed women to compare themselves to each other more easily.

Around that time, insurance companies began performing mortality
studies that showed higher death rates for overweight people. From
those studies, the standardized height-weight tables were born. After
World War II, middle-class expectations about food and fitness continued to change, and in the later years of the twentieth century the
changes escalated. These forces have had more of an effect on women

than men, but unfortunately men are now catching up. Brumberg summarizes our dilemma:

> We are faced with an abundance of food which, in our obesophobic society, necessitates ever greater self-control. On a daily basis many of us struggle with an essential contradiction in our economic system—that is, that hedonism and discipline must coexist. Middle-class Americans feel this tension most acutely in the realm of personal eating behavior. It is no wonder, then, that we talk so incessantly about food and dieting.

This "essential contradiction" is visible in any women's magazine, where advertisements for extravagant and rich foods are juxtaposed with articles about diet and fitness. This obsessive tug of war between self-indulgence and discipline is the exact opposite of the freedom Jesus desires for us. For many of us, instead of experiencing space for God, our minds are crowded with thoughts about ourselves, how we look and what we should and shouldn't eat.

MEN AND WOMEN WHO FAST

This bizarre history of food, dieting and fasting impacts both men and women as they seek to engage in Christian fasting. As I did the research for this book, I talked to more than sixty people who fast or used to fast and more than thirty people who have never engaged in fasting. The patterns among the male and female respondents were distinctly different.

The men I interviewed either fast or don't fast. Those who don't fast are simply not interested in doing so, and nearly all those who do fast engage in fasts from all food, consuming only water or juice. The women, on the other hand, are all over the map. Some fast from food. Some fast from things other than food. Like the men, some don't fast at all, but many of those women used to fast and then quit for various reasons.

Many of the women used to engage in fasts from all food but now fast from things like media and shopping and chocolate. Some of them quit fasting from food because it "puts me in a diet place, not a God place." Some of them quit because of headaches. Some felt it just wasn't helpful. Some quit when they became pregnant, and when they tried to start fasting from all food again years later, they found their bodies just didn't tolerate it very well.

Some of the female respondents simply never fast from all food because they have a history of eating disorders, and they know how dangerous it would be for them. Their concern is reinforced by Gretchen's story. A mom in her forties, Gretchen remembers a fast from all food that she undertook as a young adult. For her, that fast opened the door to bulimia. The bulimia itself lasted a year, but it took many years after that to gain emotional healing. As a result, Gretchen has been very careful to avoid fasting from food.

Aaron, a scientist in his late thirties, remembers the early days of his marriage. "My wife and I used to fast together, but she threw up every time, and that ruined the experience. I guess there are some people who, for physical reasons, just shouldn't fast from all food." According to the patterns among the many people who talked to me about fasting, women are more likely to suffer physically when fasting from all food, probably because of physiological reasons as well as the greater impact our diet culture has on women.

Of the dozens of women who shared their fasting stories with me, only a small number engage in fasts from all food, consuming only water or juice. None of those women who are able to fast successfully from all food have struggled with an eating disorder, dieted very much or worried much about their weight.

For many women and for some men, fasting from food as a Christian discipline creates significant challenges. In fact, for people with eating disorders, fasting from food is downright dangerous. For others, fasting from food can tap into our culture's obsession with dieting and thinness. If we are to rediscover a distinctively Christian form of fasting that is appropriate in our day, we have to take into account the forces at work in our lives and in our culture.

MEN AND FASTING: GOD'S STRENGTH, OUR WEAKNESS

Dale, a college student who frequently fasts from all food, says, "Fasting is really more about weakness than hunger." He sees clearly that when he allows himself to experience weakness, he opens himself to experience God's strength.

For many men, fasting from all food provides a unique opportunity they may not have anywhere else. Our culture emphasizes strength and competence, power and control, particularly for men. Fasting from all food enables men—and some women as well—to let go of their own strength and experience God's strength in their weakness.

The apostle Paul often reflected on the significance of weakness, seeing it as a way to learn that all power comes from God. Paul likens knowing Christ to a valuable treasure within our limited and finite bodies, which are like jars of the simplest pottery: "We have this treasure in clay jars, so that it may be made clear that this extraordinary power belongs to God and does not come from us" (2 Cor 4:7).

> *I've found that fasting brings clarity in prayer. This is partly because in my weakness He is strong, and partly because by setting aside my needs I can pray better.*

AARON,
A SCIENTIST IN HIS THIRTIES

Fasting from food demands—and facilitates—an integration of mind, body and spirit that connects with deep spiritual realities. Men in our culture are often disassociated from their physical bodies except in the areas of strength, fitness or sexuality. Fasting from food can open new doors to bring together the spiritual self and the physical body.

Both men and women need to experiment carefully with forms of fasting to see what works best to create space for God. According to my research, people who have seldom struggled with food, weight or frequent dieting are more likely to benefit from engaging in fasts that eliminate all food. People who have a history of problem eating or dieting are more likely to need to experiment widely with different forms of fasting to find what works for them.

A DIET PLACE OR A GOD PLACE?

My experience with fasting from food illustrates some of the issues I have just described. I have fasted from all food, drinking only water, about a dozen times. These fasts lasted for a day, a few days or a week. Every time I fasted from all food, I experienced spiritual benefit. I prayed more fervently for the poor, I felt thankful to God for all the daily gifts I received, and I mourned my habitual lack of gratitude for God's generosity to me.

However, my primary motivation for each of those fasts was to lose weight. The words of the prophet Zechariah, speaking the words of God, challenge me deeply: "When you fasted . . . was it for me that you fasted?" (Zech 7:5). I have to answer, *No, I fasted for myself. I wanted to lose weight, and I thought that fasting might have some spiritual benefit along with the weight loss.*

I've always been interested in fasting and convinced of its effectiveness, yet so many other spiritual disciplines have had more impact in my life. Sabbath keeping, contemplative prayer and intentional thankfulness have changed my life and taught me deep things about God, but fasting has been less influential over the long term.

I can see clearly that my view of fasting from food was too limited. I felt there were only two options: giving up one thing for Lent or eating no food and drinking only water. I am such a perfectionist, wanting to do things the most stringent way possible, so I never tried variations, like drinking juice when I fasted from food. I never tried fasts that involve eating a more simple diet (like a "Daniel fast" or an Eastern Orthodox fast, which we will explore in chapter six).

While my perfectionism and my narrow picture of fasting limited its benefits, a bigger issue was the way fasting lured me into the culture's obsession with dieting and thinness. *Maybe this is a spiritual technique that will also help me lose some weight so I can look better. Great. I'd better try it.* Jesus says we cannot serve two masters (Mt 6:24). In my attempts to fast from food, I was serving two masters. Fasting is powerful enough that I still obtained some spiritual benefit. But my ability to grow spiritually was limited because fasting from all food drew me into "a diet place" rather than "a God place."

Fasting, at its core, is not a discipline of withholding. Fasting is a discipline of making space for God.

Fasting, at its core, is not a discipline of withholding. Fasting is a discipline of making space for God. If a practice puts us in a place of obsessing about food or weight, then we are not creating space for God, and we are missing the central point. If that happens, we need to step back and do some groundwork in God's company, asking, "Why do I want to do this? Is there another way I can fast and pay more attention to you? And, Lord, please heal me in the area of food."

Because dieting holds such a prominent place in American life and because so many of us have a difficult relationship with food, most women and some men need to approach fasting from food very carefully. My water-only fasts were like running a marathon without any training. I dove right into the most challenging form of fasting without trying simpler forms first, and as a result the benefits of fasting were severely limited for me.

A NEW FAST: "VOLUNTARY DENIAL OF SOMETHING"

Let's look again at our definition of fasting from the first chapter and explore it further. Christian fasting is the voluntary denial of something for a specific time, for a spiritual purpose, by an individual, family, community or nation.

In the Bible and at certain times in Christian history, to fast meant to refrain from all food. When we use this narrow definition of fasting, many people should be excluded: pregnant or breastfeeding women, diabetics, people with a history of eating disorders, people on many kinds of prescription medication and people with many kinds of medical conditions for whom a strict fast might exacerbate disease symptoms.

Using a broader definition of fasting—refraining from all or some foods or refraining from other forms of gratification—anyone can fast. Today Christians fast from TV and news media, email and other kinds of technology, shopping, novels, music and using the car, in addition to various kinds of fasts from food.

These new forms of fasting make sense in our time. In years past, food was one of the only aspects of daily life considered to be necessary to human existence. In addition, mealtime was one of the great pleasures of each day as well as the major occasion for families and communities to gather. In our consumer culture, we have come to see many other things as "necessary," and we have many other daily pleasures and places to gather.

Today we can also "feast" in ways that involve so much more than food—an all-day movie extravaganza, a TV "feast" during the Olympics, a big shopping trip—so it makes sense to build a fasting-feasting rhythm into many more areas of life. In biblical times, fasting and feasting created a significant rhythm. In a nonverbal and nonanalytical way, that rhythm speaks significant truths about God's love deep into the human heart, and we will continue to see the impact of that rhythm throughout this book.

"FOR A SPECIFIC TIME"

Fasting lasts only for a set time, a season. Some people fast one day a week. Some fast during Lent, the six and a half weeks before Easter. Others fast once a month or once a year or when a prayer need is intense. The length of a fast can range from a few hours to one week or longer. Forty days is a common length for a fast because Moses, Elijah and Jesus fasted for forty days. Whatever the length, Christian fasting is always for a season only. If we refrain from doing something indefinitely or permanently, it is not fasting.

I don't eat chocolate because it gives me headaches. I learned about this connection during several Lenten fasts when I gave up chocolate and miraculously had very few headaches. However, I loved chocolate very much. So I decided year after year that I could live with headaches as long as I could consume my beloved chocolate.

Eight years ago I knew the time had come. I knew it was truly stupid to continue to eat chocolate and get so many headaches. I knew I was dealing with addictive behavior, and I was finally willing to face it, so I gave up chocolate forever. I've had only three bites of chocolate in the last eight years, once by accident and twice on purpose. To my surprise, it doesn't even taste good to me anymore. Is this a fast? No. It began as a fast, but now it has become a permanent choice, a part of my lifestyle.

Many people have made truly admirable decisions to change their lifestyles. Some of these changes originated in fasts. Several people told me they gave up TV for Lent, found they didn't miss it very much and ultimately gave away their TVs. One man gave up his car and now bikes everywhere because of his concern for the environment, and another family gave up having pets because they would rather give the money that would be spent on them to the poor.

These admirable lifestyle choices deserve a book of their own, but this is not that book. The impact of fasting comes from the unexpectedness of doing something different. During a fast, when we catch ourselves moving toward that habitual food or source of entertainment, we remind ourselves that God is more precious to us than anything else. We are reminded to pray. The unexpectedness of our temporary choices during a fast jolts us, surprises us and wakes us up.

"FOR A SPIRITUAL PURPOSE"

Many diverse groups of people encourage fasting, but a Christian fast is only for a spiritual purpose. Fasting has been popularized in recent years in the natural health movement. Various detoxification programs involve refraining from specific foods and eating other foods or supplements. The goal is health, and some people have found significant benefits from this form of fasting. Certainly God cares how we treat our bodies, perhaps more than we acknowledge, but Christian fasting is not primarily about physical health.

Mahatma Gandhi and many others throughout history have worked for political change through fasting and hunger strikes. These individuals have much to teach us about peaceful resistance and the high cost of acting on our beliefs. Certainly God desires that our faith would inform our political actions, but hunger strikes differ from Christian fasting because their goal relates to political change rather than spiritual purposes.

Some people attempt to lose weight through fasting, and this is not Christian fasting either. In fact, it is important not to focus on possible weight loss but rather on the Christ-centered purpose of the fast. In addition, Christian fasting is not a spiritualized reason to justify eating disorders.

Christian fasting is for a spiritual purpose only. The goal is to draw near to God in prayer. Motives matter in just about everything we do, but in fasting

The motivation—the reason for fasting—really does make a difference to the Lord.

CAROLINE, A HOMEMAKER
IN HER FIFTIES

our motives and purposes are absolutely vital. When a fast slides toward the goal of losing weight or manipulating God into doing what we want because of our great exercise of discipline, we have lost the heart of Christian fasting.

Time after time in both the Old and New Testaments, people prayed when they fasted. In chapter five we will look at fasting in the Bible, and we will see that when Moses, Elijah, David, Esther, Jesus and the apostles fasted, they also prayed. Intimacy with God through prayer lies behind all Christian fasting.

ONE MORE REASON

At the beginning of this chapter we considered two reasons why fasting fell out of favor with many Christians in the twentieth century. First, consumerism encourages us to believe that every desire must be met right now. Second, all too often cutting back on food puts us in a diet mode rather than a place where prayer comes more easily.

A third factor has influenced our understanding of the Christian discipline of fasting, particularly in the United States: the deeply rooted American love of positive thinking. We can see this very clearly in *The Power of Positive Thinking* by Norman Vincent Peale, a book that has been selling strongly for many decades.

Fasting draws us into intercessory prayer for the poor and needy of the world, people who are suffering in both the material and spiritual sense. On the surface, identifying with the poor does not appear to be positive. When we fast we often mourn for our own sins and the brokenness of the world, which draws us into sadness, not positive thinking.

However, fasting is rooted in true Christian positive thinking, which the Bible calls hope (Rom 5:1-5). Jesus says that Christians will fast because we long for him, the Bridegroom, to come again (Mk 2:18-20). When we fast we enter into the brokenness and emptiness that we find in this life, which increases our longing for the Bridegroom's coming.

When we fast we affirm our certainty that only in Jesus can the world be made whole. Henri Nouwen makes the connection between freedom and our hope in Christ: "Hope is the trust that God will fulfill God's promises to us in a way that leads us to true freedom. . . . The person of hope lives in the moment with the knowledge and trust that all of life is in good hands."

When we fast, we throw ourselves on the mercy of God. We acknowledge that we have nothing without God, we are utterly dependent on God, and God alone is our treasure and our hope. The freedom we experience in fasting comes from stepping outside human wisdom and human strength.

As we continue to explore Christian fasting in this book, we will look again at this paradoxical reality expressed in fasting: that as we embrace a kind of emptiness in fasting, we experience fullness and hope in Jesus Christ.

WHO SHOULD FAST?

If you desire to make more space in your life for God, if you would like to deepen your prayer life, fasting can be very helpful. Look at your life. What activities are crowding out prayer? What activities or foods are becoming more important to you than God? Is something in your life taking up more space than you want it to? What activities are siphoning off time, money or energy in a way that isn't necessarily sinful but isn't helpful either? Consider fasting from that activity or that food for a day or a few days. Ask God to help your fast create more space for him.

Fasting allows me to be in a place where I am aware of the many blessings I have in my life.

BRENT, A TEACHER
IN HIS THIRTIES

If you would like to grow in thankfulness and experience heartfelt gratitude for the blessings in your life, fasting is a helpful discipline. If you would like to pray more fervently for someone who is ill, the poor or those in need of the gospel, fasting helps. If you know you are being sucked into our consumer culture, fasting creates a small oasis of time and space for God's truth and grace to surround us.

If you have a specific prayer request weighing on your heart, fasting will almost certainly help focus those prayers. If you are not entirely sure how to pray for that need, fasting will help you make space to read the Bible, and it will enable you to listen to God for guidance in how to pray. Fasting will help deepen your prayers, add power to your prayers and remind you to pray.

Who should fast? Anyone who wants to draw near to God. The method will vary for each of us according to our diverse needs. Some people need to fast from food very carefully. Some people need to experiment gently and lightly with forms that work well for them. If we use the broadest definition—voluntary denial of something for a specific time, for a spiritual purpose, by an individual, family, community or nation—anyone can fast.

QUESTIONS FOR REFLECTION, JOURNALING AND DISCUSSION

1. Have you ever experienced an eating disorder? Have you dieted, worried about your weight or engaged in compulsive eating? Spend some time considering the possible ways you could experiment with fasting without putting yourself in a "diet place" rather than a "God place."

2. Consider the ways you like to be competent, feel in control and work from a position of strength. In what ways might fasting help you rely on God's strength?

3. In what ways do you tend to be an all-or-nothing person who needs

to do everything perfectly the first time? Think through the obstacles you might experience in starting to fast in a small way.

FOR PRAYER

Ask God to help you explore the obstacles to fasting that you might face. Ask God to guide your steps to a small beginning.

3

MOTIVES

Yet even now, says the LORD,

return to me with all your heart,

with fasting, with weeping, and with mourning;

rend your hearts and not your clothing.

Return to the LORD, your God,

for he is gracious and merciful,

slow to anger and abounding in steadfast love,

and relents from punishing.

JOEL 2:12-13

Vincent, a paralegal in his fifties, fasts in difficult situations when no solution comes to mind or when all possible solutions seem futile. He fasts from all food, drinking only water. His fasts last one day to one week—"the greater the problem, the longer the fast." He tries to be sensitive to the Holy Spirit's guidance for when and how long to fast. Vincent has been fasting in this way since he was a young adult, and many times God has guided him clearly during a fast.

Lisa, a teacher in her thirties, suffered from an eating disorder when she was younger, so she never fasts from food. Instead she fasts from other things, most commonly lattes and shopping for clothes. She says, "Denying myself something that I use for comfort is a great reminder of my desire to keep my relationship with God as my first and foremost priority. Fasting challenges me to keep a perspective of who I'm living for at all times of the day. It's great to abstain from a daily pleasure that will prompt me to regain that perspective."

We have considered some of the obstacles to fasting in our time, and we have looked at a definition of fasting that addresses some of those obstacles. In this chapter we will engage with fasting stories of real people like Vincent and Lisa. We will get a glimpse into the motivations of those who practice this ancient spiritual discipline. The connection between fasting and prayer occurs frequently in the Bible and in Christian history, which we will explore in chapters five and six. We will begin here by hearing stories about the variety of ways this discipline draws us into prayer.

A PARTNER TO PRAYER

One man who fasts regularly says, "Fasting turbocharges my prayers." A woman who frequently fasts believes it is a "sidekick to prayer," a partner to prayer. Another man says, "I believe there is a kind of clarity that comes into our prayer life when we both pray and fast."

Curt and Marlene, in their late thirties, have worked as campus pastors their whole careers. They have weathered many crises and difficult situations at work, and they have sat through countless meetings brainstorming solutions with colleagues. In recent years they have changed the way they approach challenging situations.

In the past when a difficulty or obstacle arose, they would spend a lot of time talking about options. Now they spend a day praying and fasting from food before they begin any discussion. They seek to listen to God for guidance. They have found that brainstorming solutions in staff meetings has a totally different flavor after they have fasted and prayed.

The purpose of Christian fasting is not to manipulate God into doing what we want. Fasting enables us to listen, so we hear God's direction in how to pray. In addition, for many people fasting enables more frequent prayers.

Kristen, in her midtwenties, says, "When I fast I often target a specific need or person as the focus of my prayers. That way, whenever I feel hungry I can use those cravings as a reminder to pray for the need."

Trent, in his forties, is a missionary in Asia. He heard so many miracle stories from Asian Christians about fasting that he was motivated to fast when some challenging situations came up in his work. He learned that for him, fasting is the best way to nurture prayer. When Trent fasts, he eats no food and drinks only water. He has engaged in fasts of various lengths, up to twenty days. He never feels good when he fasts; in fact he says he gets pretty crabby. But God enables him to pray much more frequently and powerfully. Even though he doesn't enjoy the process, God has spoken to Trent so clearly that he continues to turn to fasting when he needs to pray.

A few years ago Trent noticed his twelve-year-old son was getting into a bad crowd of friends, and he had no idea how to respond. He decided his best response would be to pray. He reflects, "Because I don't experience much discipline in my prayer life, that meant fasting. For three

Fasting is not the means by which we are somehow turned into Aladdin and God is turned into our compliant genie, sent to grant our every wish. We must not think that by not eating we can have God eating out of our hand.

PHIL,
A MINISTER IN HIS FORTIES

years I fasted one day almost every week for my kids." As he prayed about his son's peers over the next few months, he noticed a complete turnover of friendships. His son's new friends were all Christians, and they built a supportive community with each other that helped them weather the difficult teen years.

Several years later Trent learned that his son had seriously considered suicide when he was twelve. His son remembers that time as a turning point in his faith. Trent is so grateful he felt led to pray and fast during that time.

MAKING SPACE FOR PRAYER

Many people fast when they can't figure out any other way to cope with something very difficult. At the beginning of this chapter we heard from Vincent, who fasts when he experiences "great problems." A woman in her fifties says she fasts when she experiences "extreme needs that do not seem to yield to 'normal' prayer." A man in his forties says he fasts "around occasions of intense prayer needs."

Alan, in his forties, fasted one day a week for a year to pray for his daughter's special needs. He has observed that fasting "certainly creates time and space for more intimacy with God. I learned from fasting that there is so much God wants me to know, simply by listening rather than talking to him. As I fast, he may not reveal a specific truth or answer a prayer, but he shows me that it is a spiritually positive thing to dedicate time to being alone with him. For fasting to be meaningful, one must use the normal eating time to be with God, not simply skip meals."

Emily echoes Alan's emphasis on using a fast to make space for prayer. About eight years ago Emily, who is now in her fifties and is at home with her foster child, fasted three times for forty days as part of a Youth With A Mission emphasis on world evangelization. She fasted from all food but drank water, juice and broth. The first fast was spiritually refreshing and created great joy in her, and she felt that her ability to listen to God improved greatly. In contrast, the second and third fasts were much less satisfying.

The difference between the first fast and the other two was very simple. During the first one, Emily spent her lunch hour at work praying in her car, and she also prayed more often over the dinner hour. Her co-workers gave her a hard time about missing the social connections over lunch, so for the second and third fasts she sat in the lunchroom with her colleagues and drank her juice or broth while chatting.

Emily reflects on her experience: "It's not so much what you give up when you fast, but what you replace it with. You can just give things up and become austere. That's not the point of fasting." Fasting creates space in our lives, and Alan and Emily saw clearly that this space needs to be dedicated to prayer in order for fasts to fulfill their purpose.

PRAYING FOR HEALING

Many Christians fast before they engage in praying for healing. One woman, an elder in her congregation, always blocks out time for praying and fasting from food on the Saturday before those Sundays she is assigned to be available to pray for people in need after the worship service.

It seems counterintuitive on the surface of it, but people who fast while praying for healing report that rather than being distracted by hunger, their personal concerns seem to fade away during the fast. The fast is somehow a declaration: This thing I'm praying for is so important that I'm willing to set aside my everyday life—including food—to focus on praying for it. Fasting nurtures purity of heart and clears out the distractions of our lives. Fasting enables us to pray in a focused way for other people's healing, and we are less likely to feel absorbed or sidetracked by our own needs as we pray for others.

In a mysterious but powerful way, fasting affirms our utter dependence on God for any act of healing. Fasting also indicates our willingness to listen to God for direction in how to pray for healing.

When we fast in connection with prayers for healing, we are acknowl-
edging that life consists of much more than we can see or taste or touch.
We are affirming the power of the spiritual realm, and we are indicating
our submission to Christ as the Lord of the spiritual realm.

Gwen, a mother in her late thirties, has a powerful memory of the
connection between fasting and praying for healing. Gwen always
wanted to have four children. After her first two sons were well into their
toddler and preschool years, she and her husband started trying to get
pregnant. She had two miscarriages, one after the other, both of them
emotionally painful and hard to bear.

Then she got pregnant again. Nothing was healthy about this pregnancy. All her blood tests were outside normal range, and her physician
told her she had an autoimmune disorder that would cause her to lose
the baby. Gwen's father had just died. His death, coupled with the two
miscarriages, left Gwen feeling raw and fragile. She didn't know how she
would cope with losing yet another child.

She called Susan, an elder in her congregation who was known as a
prayer warrior. Gwen asked Susan if she would come and pray for emotional strength for Gwen to face the pain and sorrow ahead. Susan
brought oil, anointed Gwen and prayed for her, as commanded in James
5:14.

Susan began by praying for the strength that Gwen had asked for. But
Susan went on to pray for complete healing of the autoimmune disorder
in Gwen's body. She prayed for a healthy pregnancy and for future
healthy pregnancies. She prayed for healing in a way that Gwen couldn't
pray for herself.

When Susan prayed, Gwen felt something change in her body. She
didn't want to say anything about the sensation to Susan or to her husband, so she just waited. A week later, at her next appointment with the
doctor, her blood tests were normal. The doctor said it was a miracle.

Gwen's miracle baby is now a healthy and lively four-year-old, and his younger brother is healthy as well.

Susan, a woman experienced in praying for healing, fasted from food before she came to Gwen's house to pray for her. Along with the fasting, Susan prayed ahead of time for guidance in how to focus her prayers for Gwen. Susan felt led by God to pray for Gwen's total healing, not just for the strength to face another miscarriage.

Gwen reflects, "Miraculous healing is a part of the Christian experience. I pray for it and I encourage others to pray for it. It's an important element that is missing in many Christian traditions." For many Christians, fasting is a significant part of praying for healing, bringing power, clarity and focus to our prayers and enabling us to hear God's direction for our prayers.

What about those times when we commit to fast and pray for healing, and God doesn't answer our prayers? Do we reach a point where we stop asking God for healing? Sometimes—in fact, quite often—when God doesn't answer our prayers in the way we desire, God is working in the situation in a different way than we expect.

Fasting makes us more attentive to God's hand in any situation. Because fasting helps us listen to God, we are often more able to see God's answers that don't fall into our preconceived patterns.

MAKING SPACE FOR GOD

Dale, a college student, fasts because he wants to commune with God more intimately. He says, "I fast because it empties me of myself, my own strivings and ambitions, and it makes more space within myself to receive from the Lord."

Dale is motivated by Matthew 9:15, where Jesus talks about fasting and calls himself the Bridegroom. Jesus says, "The days will come when the bridegroom is taken away," and in those days we will be motivated to fast. Dale meditates on this verse. He says, "I picture Jesus holding his arms wide open and inviting me to know him more and receive more of him into myself."

Audrey, also a college student, is motivated by her hunger for more of the Lord. She says, "Growing in Christ is a process that takes time, but fasting and prayer act as a catalyst that speeds it up. At times I fast to pray for specific needs, but mostly I do what I call 'lovesick' fasts. Every time I fast, I am amazed at how much time I have to seek the Lord just by excluding mealtimes from my daily routine. Fasting causes me to dwell on the faithfulness and strength of the Lord, as well as humble myself before him in voluntary weakness. God always draws near to the humble, and I love experiencing his tenderness and grace in that place of weakness."

For Audrey, fasting "tenderizes my heart toward the Lord. My spirit becomes all the more sensitive to his promptings, his voice, his touch."

ROUNDING OUT OUR PRAYERS

Fasting helps us pray in new ways. We may be good at praying for the needs of our family but not the needs of people in other parts of the world. We may find that we are thankful for some things but not others. We may feel sorry and repentant for the same things over and over. Fasting often opens up new paths in prayer, particularly in the areas of thankfulness, repentance and remembering the needs of the poor and hungry.

Teresa, a mom with six-year-old twins, has experienced richness in prayer through fasting. Since becoming a mom, she has fasted mostly from things other than food, but she still fondly remembers one significant Lenten fast from food about fifteen years ago. She felt led that year to fast from twenty-four hours of meals once each week, beginning with dinner and continuing through breakfast and lunch the next day. She let herself drink whatever she wanted, including lattes and an occasional milk shake.

Teresa remembers,

> I began to wake up on the mornings after missing dinner with an overwhelming sense of gratitude for things I had so taken for granted. I'm sure I never thought to thank God for them. It happened in that twilight when one is just awaking, but before conscious thoughts creep in. I would find myself literally basking in the warmth of flannel sheets on a cool morning, grateful to God that I had a cozy room in a cozy home, a soft bed, warm sheets, a furnace that produced heat, food to look forward to later when I would break the fast. I am not a morning person, so it was not the time of day when I usually prayed; therefore this was something new and unexpected. It was lovely to begin my day with spontaneous and heartfelt prayers of gratitude, which was an attitude that began to characterize that entire Lent, even on nonfasting days. Along with it came a conviction of my sin of ungratefulness. I had thought of myself as a grateful person, but that Lent showed me just how much I take for granted in my rich, Western life. I was much more aware of those for whom cold and hunger is a reality in their lives, not something they choose as a part of a fast.

My own experience with fasting from food closely parallels Teresa's. As I mentioned earlier, I have fasted from all food about a dozen times, drinking only water. Those fasts have ranged in length from one day to one week. When I fast from all food, I am so much more aware of how incredibly blessed I am to have food on the table every day. Taking away food helps me notice the abundance of what God has given me: food, a family, a home, a car, clothes to wear, books to read, interesting work. I become deeply aware of how ungrateful I am most of the time. Fasting from food also gives me a brief time of solidarity with the hungry around the world, and I find myself praying much more frequently for justice

Fasting is a small way of walking with those who suffer from hunger.

CHARLOTTE, A RETIRED
TEACHER IN HER SEVENTIES

for the poor and for people who serve the poor in Christ's name.

I have also engaged in nonfood fasts, particularly during Lent. For the past five years I have repeated the same Lenten fast because it has been so rich and meaningful. I give up all my colorful jewelry and wear a silver cross necklace every day. The cross focuses me on Christ's death and resurrection and the freedom and forgiveness I receive through his obedience. During Lent I find myself thanking God much more often than usual for Christ's work on the cross.

Giving up colorful jewelry for six and a half weeks sounds trivial, but year after year it speaks to me of the sacrifice Jesus made to come to earth. I give up a small pleasure, but Jesus gave up so much more. "For you know the generous act of our Lord Jesus Christ, that though he was rich, yet for your sakes he became poor, so that by his poverty you might become rich" (2 Cor 8:9). Jesus left the splendor of heaven, with its bright colors and beauty infinitely more intense than my cheerful jewelry, because he loves us. During Lent I find myself thanking God frequently for sending Jesus to earth.

Fasting opens up our prayer life by helping us notice what we haven't been thankful for. As we thank God in new ways, we are often led directly into repentance and prayers for people who suffer and lack so many of the basic necessities of life.

Fasting reminds us to pray, enables us to pray and grounds our prayers in intimacy with God. Fasting enables us to hear God's voice in prayer. Prayer is the primary motivation for Christian fasting. Several secondary motivations for fasting have been common throughout Christian history, and we will consider those now.

OTHER REASONS TO FAST

Lauren Winner, author of *Girl Meets God* and *Real Sex,* began to fast one day a week because her minister stressed fasting so strongly. On her fast day she drinks juices and eats no food. She writes that she is "not a big fan of fasting," but she is also beginning to realize some of the benefits. "I'm beginning to see that I recognize my dependence on God more clearly when I'm hungry; I'm beginning to chip away at some of the stupor that comes with always being sated. . . . What fasting is slowly teaching me is the simple lesson that I am not utterly subject to my bodily desires."

In the face of strong messages from our culture that say we should satisfy every desire as soon as we feel it, fasting teaches us something countercultural and deeply significant for our life of faith. The apostle Paul, in his first letter to the Corinthians, uses the metaphor of athletes in a race: "Athletes exercise self-control in all things," Paul writes (1 Cor 9:25). Just as athletes exercise self-discipline and don't give in to every desire that sweeps across their minds, shouldn't Christians discipline themselves for the sake of a greater goal than winning an athletic contest?

Throughout history, Christians have known that fasting teaches the body obedience, which helps us draw near to God more fully. Christians have also known that fasting makes feast days more joyous. The practice of Lenten fasts arose because of a desire to identify with Christ in his sufferings but also to celebrate the joy of Easter with greater enthusiasm.

Corinne, in her fifties, fasts during Lent. She says, "It makes the resurrection have a physical connection to me because I have suffered in a tiny way, and I do mean tiny, during Lent. When I fast from something during Lent, I enjoy Easter more."

Peter, in his forties, fasts for two days

Those who would enjoy

the feast

should fast on the eve.

ITALIAN PROVERB

before Thanksgiving and two days before Easter, "in preparation for gratitude and joy." Joel, also in his forties, fasted from coffee once during Lent. He concluded it was a big mistake because of the headaches from caffeine withdrawal and the lack of energy throughout Lent, but he remembers "a very great Easter!"

Fasting helps us experience solidarity with those who don't have enough to eat. Skipping a meal frees up money to give to the poor, as Christians have known throughout history and still experience today. Organizations such as World Vision, Oxfam and Catholic Relief Services are doing a terrific job bringing this kind of fasting into prominence in Western countries. World Vision, for example, offers a program called the Thirty Hour Famine, in which participants fast from food as a group for thirty hours. They recruit sponsors for each hour of the fast to raise money for the poor. Throughout the thirty hours, participants see videos and discuss world poverty, spend time in worship and prayer for the poor, and engage in service to their communities.

A Seattle church youth group has participated in the Thirty Hour Famine several times. Recently they added a new twist. The famine took place in the church's youth center, but the juice and water were kept several blocks away on the front porch of a congregation member's house. As the group walked several blocks many times during the thirty hours, they felt connected in a small way to the poor of the world, many of whom have to walk a long way to draw water from a well. This helped make poverty feel real and fueled both prayer and generosity for people who experience hunger.

OUR TRUE HUNGER

Another reason to fast is to listen to what is truly inside us. Lauren Winner writes, "Fasting is not meant to drag us down, but to still us. It is not meant to distract us from the really real, but rather to silence us so that we can hear things as they most truly are." Because time goes more slowly while fasting and we step outside our daily routines and habits, we have time to notice those inner voices we usually miss.

As we take the time to listen to the inner voices we so often ignore, we are more able to come into God's presence in honesty and vulnerability. The apostle Paul tells us to "present your bodies as a living sacrifice" (Rom 12:1), and we are more able to do this because we know more accurately who we are as we offer ourselves to God.

Mark, a consultant in his sixties, reflects, "What I've learned from fasting is that it is often difficult to know that for which we are hungry when we are satiated all the time. We actually need to experience physical hunger in order to trace what our real spiritual and emotional hunger is."

Barry, a pastor in his forties, agrees. "In a society that tries to mask and cover up all hunger, it is important to get in touch with our real hunger. We take so many anesthetics to mask our hunger. We need to remove those masks."

What is my true hunger? In what ways am I satisfying myself too easily with toys and mindless pleasures? What does my desire for God really look like? These are some of the questions we may find ourselves considering when we fast, and the answer to these questions will nourish our life of prayer.

Embracing Emptiness

Warning: People who refrain from food or from media, information and entertainment need to be willing to encounter emptiness. In order to make space both to listen to our inner voices and to hear God's word to us, first we have to create an empty space.

Gerald May points out that human beings have trouble with empty spaces. We are addicted, May writes, "to filling up every kind of space we encounter. We are addicted to fulfillment, to the eradication of all emptiness." In addition, "we fear what spaciousness will reveal to us. We would rather have the anesthetized serenity of dullness than the liberating dis-ease of truth. Together our addiction to fulfillment and our flight from truth weave a harsh, desperate barrier against participation in love."

Our addiction to filling space and our discomfort with truth make the discipline of fasting challenging. A pervasive cultural myth says that if we are well-adjusted people, we will be happy all the time. A common religious myth tells us a similar lie—that God will make everything easy and peaceful. These myths have impressed on our hearts the lie that if we are experiencing discomfort, we're doing something wrong or God has abandoned us.

Just as our worst side is revealed when we're hungry, lonely and tired . . . fasting reveals the things that control us, the parts of ourselves we'd hoped would go away.

JAN JOHNSON,
FASTING AND SIMPLICITY

Fasting involves discomfort, sometimes the physical discomfort of hunger, other times the discomfort of disregarding our desire for media or shopping or some other treat. Our culture tells us that discomfort indicates something is wrong. Yet as we fast, we affirm the opposite. Fasting acts out our commitment to the belief that there is more to life than transitory fulfillment of the moment's needs or wants. Ultimately fasting affirms that God loves us and desires that we draw near to him.

Because fasting is so profoundly countercultural, it may feel uncomfortable at first. We may find inner voices conducting an argument inside our minds and hearts. Some voices will say that we need to rush to meet every need right now: God wants us to experience the abundant life; we are crazy to deny ourselves anything! Other voices say that self-denial is a form of punishment, and we are so worthless we deserve to be punished. Other voices may say God desires that we suffer, so God must not love us.

When we fast, we open ourselves up to these voices and lies. We enter into a spiritual battle. Countering the lies with God's truth takes a lot of effort. Most people who fast emphasize the Bible as a key ingredient in a spiritually healthy fast. When we fast we have more time both for prayer and for reading the Bible. The truth of the Bible helps us find God's voice in the empty spaces created by fasting.

We can continue to numb ourselves with a fast-paced life and endless indulgences. Or we can embrace the challenge of creating space that might feel uncomfortable at times but will deepen our capacity for rich joy and powerful prayer. Fasting brings us that challenge.

WHY FAST? WHY NOW?

Fasting makes space for God. Nagging hunger pangs, feeling crabby or longing for candy or our favorite TV show can remind us to pray. When we give up something small, we are reminded of Jesus' much greater sacrifice for us.

Fasting connects us with the poor of the world. As the AIDS crisis in Africa is making news and as Western countries are considering how to do more to address poverty worldwide, fasting helps us pray more passionately and more frequently for the poor. Fasting gives us a small window into what it is like for so many who do without. This increases prayer, compassion and a sense of solidarity with those in need.

Fasting clears away some of the distractions of our lives so we can hear God more clearly. Because we are hearing God, we are more likely to pray for the things God wants us to pray for, so our prayers have more vigor and depth.

Most precious of all, fasting cultivates intimacy with God. It helps us discern God's will and know and experience God's love deep inside us in new ways. The fruit of fasting often lasts long after the fast is over and gives us a taste of heaven.

In our time people are longing for authenticity, particularly in their

When you fast, you stop pursuing food and the other necessities of life to passionately pursue the presence of God.

ELMER TOWNS,
THE BEGINNER'S GUIDE TO FASTING

life of faith. Fasting nurtures authenticity. Fasting helps us draw near to God honestly and thankfully because who we are and what we desire are exposed. We can give those desires to God in intercession and confession.

Fasting connects us with mystery. After decades of emphasis on scientific objectivity and cognitive reasons for faith, Christians today are learning to embrace mystery, which has been a part of Christian experience across the centuries. God does seem to answer prayer in a different way when we fast, and we can explain this mystery only in part.

Christians are ready to experience this spiritual power because we have seen that a faith based entirely on reason lacks authenticity and mystery. Fasting is a spiritual discipline that is right for our time, helping us stand against the lies of our culture and enabling us to experience in our hearts the true compassion and generosity of God.

QUESTIONS FOR REFLECTION, JOURNALING AND DISCUSSION

1. Which of the stories in this chapter are attractive to you? Why? Do any stories make you feel uneasy? Why?

2. Are you drawn to any of the ways fasting can nurture prayer?

3. Fasting can help us learn that all desires do not have to be met instantly. It can help us pray for and identify with the poor, and it can help us discover more of what is truly inside us. In what ways are these aspects of fasting attractive to you? In what ways are they uncomfortable?

4. Are you willing to embrace discomfort as you create space in your life? What would you like to learn from it?

FOR PRAYER

Spend some time praying about the ways you pray. Ask God to teach you to pray more easily and more frequently. Ask God to train you to hear his voice more as you pray. Bring your longings and fears about fasting to God.

4

A Look at
Christian History

After they had appointed elders for them in each church,
with prayer and fasting they entrusted them
to the Lord in whom they had come to believe.

ACTS 14:23

Richard Foster, in his book *Celebration of Discipline,* points out that he couldn't find a single book on the topic of Christian fasting published between 1861 and 1954, a period of almost one hundred years. He asks, "What would account for this almost total disregard of a subject so frequently mentioned in Scripture and so ardently practiced by Christians throughout the centuries?"

Foster echoes the ideas expressed in chapter two—that we are constantly bombarded by propaganda telling us we need to satisfy all our appetites as quickly as possible. We have come to believe that skipping a meal will put us on the verge of starvation. In addition to these cultural forces at work in the twentieth century, Foster notes that fasting developed a bad reputation because of excesses during the Middle Ages.

As we look at the history of Christian fasting, we will see two strands of thought that continuously reappear. One of them is healthy and biblical, and one of them is dangerous. The first strand goes like this: The physical body is a gift from God. Food, meals and fellowship around the table are also gifts from God. Sometimes we set aside God's good gifts to make space for equally good things: prayer, sacrifice and intimacy with God. In addition, we are fallen human beings, and our appetites can lead us astray. So we benefit from stepping outside our appetites for a season to put them in perspective through prayer. Fasting, in this view, teaches us valuable discipline based in God's good creation. This view acknowledges our tendency to turn away from God and affirms God's loving redemption of our whole beings—bodies and souls—in Jesus Christ.

The second strand of thought, dangerous and destructive, begins in a different place: We are totally damaged and warped because we are fallen human beings. Therefore we can't trust our bodies or our appetites—for food, for sex, for any kind of luxury—at all. We need to fight our appetites at all times because the desires of the flesh always lead us away from God. A truly spiritual Christian will fast as often as possible, eat as little as possible, enjoy as few pleasures as possible and stay unmarried and celibate.

The snapshots of fasting in the Bible that we will look at in the next chapter do not even begin to hint at this second point of view. People in the Bible stopped eating so they could pray more fervently for deliverance, guidance or protection. They fasted so they could express their deep mourning and repentance. They put away food, a normal and healthy aspect of human life, for something even more important. By fasting they acknowledged that intimacy with God is the most important thing in human life.

THE EARLY CENTURIES AFTER JESUS

The Didache, an instructional handbook for Christians that probably dates from the second century, directs Christians to fast on Wednesdays and Fridays. This text notes that the Jews fasted on Mondays and Thursdays, so these new days would establish a uniquely Christian pattern of fasting in contrast to Judaism. Wednesdays and Fridays were chosen because of their connection to the end of Jesus' life. On Wednesday Judas told the Jewish authorities where they could find Jesus the next day to arrest him, and on Friday Jesus was crucified.

Other early Christian writers—Justin Martyr, Polycarp, Hermas, Pseudo-Barnabas—frequently exhorted their readers to fast. The early Christians fasted before Easter, the biggest feast day, as a time of preparation and cleansing. They also fasted in preparation for baptism, an extremely significant event that marked acceptance into the community of faith. *The Didache* recommends that the baptizer and the baptized, and others in the congregation who are able, fast for one or two days prior to baptism. Baptisms were often held on the Saturday before Easter, confirming the significance of fasting before Easter.

Nothing is so inconsistent with the life of any Christian as overindulgence.

THE RULE OF BENEDICT,
SIXTH CENTURY

During the third century, the fast before Easter was extended to the six days of Holy Week, with the goal of mystical union with Christ. Christians during this period believed that the faithful could identify with Jesus in his suffering by fasting. The forty-day Lenten fast came into practice in the fourth century, after Christianity became the official religion of the Roman Empire under Constantine. Because the persecution of Christians ended with this change, forms of self-discipline such as fasting replaced martyrdom as a way to experience the suffering of Christ and discipline the body to bring it under control. This included partial fasts from wine or meat as well as fasts from all food.

To Help the Poor

In the early church, fasting was understood as abstinence from all food from morning until evening, and the evening meal was to be as simple as possible. In the early centuries after Christ, "simple" meant bread and water. Food that would normally have been eaten was to be given to the poor. In later years other foods were permitted, so fasting came to be the prohibition of meat and wine. By not eating these expensive foods, money was freed up to give to the poor.

This practice, advocated in Isaiah 58, was a major theme in the early years of the Christian faith. Sometime around A.D. 128, Aristide, a journalist, explained to Emperor Hadrian the way Christians lived: "When someone is poor among them who has need of help, they fast for two or three days, and they have the custom of sending him the food which they had prepared for themselves."

The *Shepherd of Hermas,* a Christian book of teachings that dates from around 150, says, "In the day on which you fast, you will taste nothing but bread and water and having reckoned up the price of the dishes of that day which you intended to have eaten, you will give it to a widow, or an orphan, or to some person in want, and thus you will exhibit humility of mind, so that the one who has received benefit from your humility may fill his own soul."

Origen blessed those who fasted to "nourish the poor." For Augustine, a bishop in North Africa from 395 to 430 and author of *Confessions,* fasting was merely avarice unless one gave away what one would have eaten. He wrote, "Break your bread for those who are hungry, said Isaiah, do not believe that fasting suffices. Fasting chastises you, but it does not refresh the other. Your

Do you wish your prayer

to fly toward God?

Give it two wings:

fasting and almsgiving.

AUGUSTINE, FIFTH CENTURY

privations shall bear fruit if you give generously to another."

This emphasis on fasting as a way to benefit the poor continued for many centuries. Gregory the Great, bishop of Rome, preached in the late sixth century that those who do not give what they save from fasting to the poor, but reserve it for their own appetite at a later time, do not fast for God.

OTHER EARLY THEMES

In the first centuries after Jesus, other themes were also connected with fasting. Fasting was viewed as a way back to paradise. In the Garden of Eden, Adam and Eve ate a limited diet of only fruits and vegetables, and they were expelled from the Garden for eating a forbidden food. This view has continued in the Eastern Orthodox churches, which embrace a form of fasting that involves eating a vegan diet.

Fasting was also viewed as a way to get nearer to God. John Chrysostom wrote, "As bodily food fattens the body, so fasting strengthens the soul; imparting it an easy flight, it makes it able to ascend on high, to contemplate lofty things and to put the heavenly higher than the pleasant and pleasurable things of life." Fasting was believed to create inner purity, a favorable condition to receive God, which explains in part the tradition of fasting to prepare for Communion and baptism.

Some early Christians were influenced by Plato, who believed that the soul was trapped in the body and we can only realize our divine potential by disentangling ourselves from the world of the senses. This led to the view in the early church that earthly desires were wicked and had to be curbed in favor of the pure soul. The result was the ideal of complete independence from physical needs. Fasting, sleep deprivation, self-flagellation and sexual abstinence were admired as ways to subdue the "sinful flesh."

We can see some of this influence in the strange words of Tertullian who advocated fasting because "an emaciated body will more readily

pass the narrow gate (of paradise), a light body will resurrect more rap-
idly, and in the grave, a wasted body will be preserved best."

Theresa Shaw, a scholar who studies the early church, writes, "The
stuff of the body, the flesh itself, weighs heavily. Jerome, writing in the
late fourth century, describes the flesh as a burden, borne along by the
spirit through its pilgrimage in this world, like bulky baggage that will
be cast off only after death. For Basil of Ancyra, the flesh tugs at the
'wings of the soul' like a leaden weight that pulls fishing nets down into
the waters."

As we step back to get an overview of the early years of the Christian
church, we see that fasting sometimes took on an overly austere flavor
that reinforced a negative view of the body. More often, though, fasting
was a positive discipline that helped people prepare for events such as
baptism and Easter. Fasting freed up money and food to give to the poor,
and it connected Christians with God's heart of compassion for those in
need. Fasting was usually viewed as a way to learn discipline and to draw
near to God with pure and open hearts.

MEDIEVAL CHRISTIANS

Literature in the medieval period gives us a mixed view of fasting.
Thomas Aquinas, in the thirteenth century, is only one example of a
Christian writer who praised moderation and gladness of heart in all
things yet also gave detailed and precise rules for fasting that seem to
convey a legalistic need to obey rules to gain God's approval.

In addition, Aquinas encouraged fasting "in order to bridle the lusts
of the flesh." This statement could be interpreted as an affirmation of
fasting as a positive and helpful discipline that teaches us not to give in
to every desire we experience. However, it could also be interpreted as a
statement that affirms the utter sinfulness of the human body. Unfortunately, Christians have all too often interpreted statements like this one
to mean that our bodies are dirty and evil in every way.

Some medieval literature seems helpful and biblical. Bonaventure, a contemporary of Aquinas, wrote about two aspects of the Christian life: the contemplative, or reflective, aspect and the active aspect, which focused on the things we do because of our faith. Bonaventure linked prayer to the contemplative aspect of the Christian life, and he connected almsgiving—generosity to the poor—to the active aspect. He believed fasting supports Christians in doing both.

In the Middle Ages fasting was viewed in the context of these words of Jesus: "If any want to become my followers, let them deny themselves and take up their cross and follow me" (Mt 16:24). This verse can inspire us today, but its meaning can also be warped into a need to earn God's approval. During the Middle Ages fasting was often viewed as a work that can help earn salvation.

Fasting was also a form of penance, a sign of remorse over sins committed by the person who fasted or by others. Sometimes this remorse took the form of healthy humility, designed to incite God's compassion, similar to the fasting of the Ninevites in the book of Jonah. Other times it became a form of self-castigation and self-punishment, based on the view that the physical body is inherently evil. This view of the body was never a part of biblical Christian beliefs, but it crept into both theology and practice. Fasting was one practice where this warped emphasis often took hold.

During the medieval period fasting became a practice of elite Christians who were viewed as especially holy. The saints who engaged in vigorous fasting were often viewed by other Christians as engaging in sacrifice for the sake of the whole church, a kind of sacrifice for everyone's sins. The fasting saints were viewed as God's chosen ones, and some female saints fasted to dangerous extremes.

Ordinary Christians also fasted, on Fridays and at Lent, especially in the form of abstinence from meat. As always, people tried to figure out exemptions to rules. Children, the ill and the elderly had always been excluded from fasting, but after the fourth century others had the opportunity to refrain from fasting. In the late medieval period the wealthy paid for indulgences and exemptions, which allowed them to eat rich food on fast days. In the thirteenth century some monks who were instructed to fast from all meat except game that had been hunted decided to get around that rule by letting their pigs loose and turning them into game.

We can see that in the Middle Ages, the practice of fasting sometimes created space for God and nurtured prayer and generosity. More often though, fasting was viewed as a set of rules designed to earn salvation, based on a negative view of the human body. And as a result, such rigid rules created the desire to get around those rules.

THE EASTERN CHURCHES

After the eleventh-century split between the Eastern Orthodox and Roman Catholic churches, Christians in Orthodox churches fasted frequently and consistently. Eastern Orthodox churches teach that the human body is not evil and that fasting has nothing to do with punishing the body. Fasting is connected to repentance as a way of restoring spiritual health and to the kind of purity humans experienced in the Garden of Eden. It prepares Christians to receive Holy Communion and baptism. Fasting is a liberating experience that reorients the human will and provides an opportunity to discipline all the body's appetites in a way that brings freedom and health.

Over the course of history, as many as 180 days have been viewed as fast days in Orthodox churches. In addition to the fasting season of Lent that comes before Easter, three other "Lents" have

> *The Christian message is that fasting strengthens us for love.*

CAROLE GARIBALDI ROGERS,
FASTING: EXPLORING A GREAT SPIRITUAL PRACTICE

been observed: the Lent of the Holy Apostles (twelve days in early summer), Mary's Lent (two weeks in late summer) and the Lent preceding Christmas (mid-November to December 24). Fasting is also observed at Epiphany, Saint John the Baptist's Day, Holy Cross Day and every Wednesday and Friday.

Orthodox fasting eliminates dairy, meat, fish, eggs, olive oil and wine. Fasting is to be taken seriously, but these rules are not to be dour or legalistic, "for the kingdom of God is not food and drink but righteousness and peace and joy in the Holy Spirit" (Rom 14:17). Eastern Orthodox Christians fast as a community, and afterward they celebrate the feasts together as well. A Russian Orthodox saying asserts, "One can be damned alone, but saved only with others." Fasting in this tradition is a corporate act, as is feasting.

THE PROTESTANT REFORMATION

Many of the reformers of the sixteenth to eighteenth centuries viewed fasting as a way to open themselves to God. In the early 1500s Martin Luther wrote, "On fasting I say this: it is right to fast frequently in order to subdue and control the body. For when the stomach is full, the body does not serve for preaching, for praying, for studying, or for doing anything else that is good. Under such circumstances God's Word cannot remain. But one should not fast with a view to meriting something by it as by a good work." Luther objected to the church setting rules about when and how to fast, and he continually emphasized that justification comes to us solely through the work of Jesus Christ, not through any discipline we exercise.

John Calvin, another prominent theologian in the mid 1500s, viewed the practice as a way to encourage prayer and to humble oneself before God. Calvin was strenuously opposed to the hypocrisy and artificial obligations of the medieval church, and he saw fasting as connected to these harmful practices, so he made no detailed recommendations about fasting.

John Wesley, founder of Methodism in the 1700s, wanted to revive the teaching of *The Didache*. He encouraged Methodists to fast on Wednesdays and Fridays. He felt so strongly about this discipline that in the early years he wouldn't ordain anyone to the Methodist ministry who didn't fast on those two days. In later years Wesley and many Methodist leaders fasted on Fridays only.

IN THE HISTORY OF NATIONS

Many early American settlers, including the Puritans, emphasized fasting. During a revival in the mid-eighteenth century, at the time of Jonathan Edwards, fasting came into prominence as a way to connect to God's power. Edwards fasted twenty-two hours before delivering his famous sermon "Sinners in the Hands of an Angry God." During the layman's prayer revival in the 1800s, people skipped lunch to pray.

Fasting also played a role in national politics. In 1774, when the British Parliament ordered an embargo on the Port of Boston, the legislative body of the State of Virginia called for a day of public humiliation, prayer and fasting. George Washington wrote in his journal that he fasted that day. In 1798, when the United States was on the verge of war with France, John Adams proclaimed a day of solemn humiliation, prayer and fasting. During the War of 1812, the two houses of Congress passed a joint resolution calling for a day of public humiliation, prayer and fasting.

During the Civil War, Abraham Lincoln called three times for a day of national humiliation, prayer and fasting. Lincoln encouraged fasting and prayer both in places of worship and in homes. Our national leaders used the word "humiliation" instead of our more familiar word "humility," but clearly the intent of these fasts was to pray humbly for God's guidance and protection in a time of national need.

Political leaders in other countries called for national days of fasting as well. In England during the Napoleonic Wars and World War II, the

It behooves us then, to humble ourselves before the offended Power, to confess our national sins, and to pray for clemency and forgiveness.

ABRAHAM LINCOLN,
PROCLAIMING A NATIONAL
FAST DAY DURING
THE CIVIL WAR

nation was invited to fast and pray. Fasting has played a role in the United States and other countries when leaders have called people to pray humbly for their nation and enhance that prayer and humility with fasting.

FOUR MOVEMENTS OF THE LATE TWENTIETH CENTURY

In the first half of the twentieth century fasting was not emphasized in Western countries as a spiritual discipline. The renaissance of fasting we are experiencing now comes from several diverse movements and individuals. These are almost completely unrelated to each other, but they have converged to bring about an emphasis on this practice to the church today.

The first significant movement was increased interest in the gifts and power of the Holy Spirit. The Pentecostal movement began in the early 1900s. In the 1960s and 1970s, this interest in the Holy Spirit spread to mainline churches in the charismatic movement. In the 1980s and 1990s, a concern for walking in the power of the Holy Spirit spread even further, into many congregations of various Christian traditions. This most recent emphasis on the Holy Spirit is sometimes called the "third wave" of the Holy Spirit's movement in the church. The spread of this movement has also widened the emphasis on fasting.

Many Christians who emphasize the Holy Spirit's gifts make a connection between fasting and the power of the Holy Spirit in healing. This is based on Matthew 17:21: "This kind goeth not out but by prayer and fasting" (Mt 17:21 KJV; see also Mk 9:29). In Pentecostal, charismatic, and third-wave churches, fasting is intimately connected with breaking

Satan's power in people's lives and bringing supernatural power to prayer.

A second influential movement has been the increased popularity of Eastern Orthodox churches. A number of prominent evangelical Christians have joined Eastern Orthodox churches, and magazines like *Christianity Today* and *The Christian Century* increasingly print articles about what other Christians can learn from the Orthodox churches. Because fasting has been an integral and positive part of congregational life in Orthodox churches and because it is free from most of the destructive excesses of fasting in the medieval Western church, both Protestants and Roman Catholics are viewing fasting in a new light.

A third factor that has brought fasting to the attention of Western Christians is greater communication with the churches in the developing world, where fasting is common. Christians in many churches in Africa, Asia, and South and Central America fast frequently and consistently as an everyday part of congregational life. People who visit these countries on short-term mission trips and vacations have heard the many miracle stories connected to fasting. The church in the developing world understands the benefits of consistent fasting in a way that Western Christians are just beginning to rediscover. We will see some examples of fasting overseas in chapter eight.

A fourth movement is the emerging leadership in the church of members of Generation X and Y, the two generations just behind the baby boomers. These younger Christians love experiential spiritual disciplines, and they believe Christians in the twentieth century have lost something by ignoring history. As a result, Gen-X and Gen-Y Christians have embraced ancient Christian disciplines such as contemplative prayer, worship involving icons, foot washing and fasting. Christians of these generations see more clearly the great loss to Christian discipleship when we neglect ancient patterns of worship and devotion, especially those practices with experiential components.

THREE INFLUENTIAL PEOPLE

In addition to these four religious movements, three individuals have promoted fasting in different and complementary ways in the last decades of the twentieth century, impacting Christians in North America and other Western countries.

In his landmark 1978 book, *Celebration of Discipline,* Richard Foster gently and vividly explores twelve classical spiritual disciplines, including meditation, submission, service, confession and fasting. Richard Foster's writing and speaking have nurtured a renewed interest in the spiritual disciplines that shaped the church for most of two millennia but which had been largely forgotten in the twentieth century.

In Foster's book the section on fasting makes the connection between fasting and prayer, discusses the reasons fasting might seem strange in our culture and states clearly that the Bible seems to assume people of faith will fast. In his book Foster discusses only fasting from food, but when he has spoken on fasting in various settings he has also acknowledged the significance of fasting from things other than food.

He who fasts and does not do good, saves his bread but loses his soul.

H. G. BOHN, *HANDBOOK OF PROVERBS,* 1855

A second person who shaped our current understanding of fasting is Mother Teresa, winner of the Nobel Peace Prize. More than any other person in recent years, she taught Christians and non-Christians alike that God is especially present when we care for the poor. Mother Teresa fasted frequently, led fasts for her followers and encouraged interfaith fasts for various causes.

Mother Teresa recommended fasting from food and also from things that cost money, freeing up funds to give to the poor. The authors of an introductory book on fasting state, "To Mother Teresa, fasting was a way to do without in order to provide more for others, a way to cleanse the spirit to be in closer contact with God, and a way to petition for social change."

The third person of note was Bill Bright, founder of Campus Crusade for Christ. Bright wrote more than fifty books and booklets, including several about fasting. In the mid-1990s, Bright began promoting forty-day fasts as a way to engage in prayer for world evangelization, targeting the year 2000 as a goal for reaching all the world with the Christian gospel.

Bright influenced many evangelical congregations and mission organizations. Between 1995 and 2000, many Christians in the United States and around the world fasted for forty days, often in community with others, to pray for the spread of the gospel and the needs of the church around the world.

These three people influenced many others to try fasting, and in their words we find some of the main themes that continue to shape the way we understand Christian fasting today. Richard Foster advocated rediscovering an ancient spiritual discipline that nurtures intimacy with God. Mother Teresa encouraged fasting in order to pray for, provide for and experience solidarity with the poor. Bill Bright emphasized fasting in order to pray for world evangelization.

Fasting results in a greater intimacy with and a deeper enthusiasm for God, which in turn spills over into every other area of life.

BILL BRIGHT,
*THE TRANSFORMING POWER
OF FASTING AND PRAYER*

The Pentecostal, charismatic and third wave movements help us remember that fasting has mysterious and miraculous power beyond what we can describe. The Eastern Orthodox churches remind us that fasting is a positive discipline, promoting spiritual health. Christians in the developing world demonstrate that fasting can be a part of everyday Christian spirituality, lived in community. Young adult Christians have reminded us of the significance of historic Christian disciplines that enable us to engage experientially with God's truth. All of these emphases are essential to understanding fasting at its best.

In the eighteenth century, John Wesley wrote, "Some have exalted religious fasting beyond all Scripture and reason; and others have utterly disregarded it." We can see in our survey of church history that indeed some have warped fasting into a discipline that denigrates the body as evil and should be continually denied. We know from our own observation that others have disregarded fasting entirely. Yet we do have many voices presenting a positive model that encourages prayer, gentle and appropriate self-denial, and generosity to the poor. We can draw on the positive models and leave the others behind.

QUESTIONS FOR REFLECTION, JOURNALING AND DISCUSSION

1. Before you read this chapter, how would you have described the role of fasting in Christian history? What did you learn here?

2. Of all the quotations cited in this chapter, which ones jumped out at you? What attracted you or made you feel uneasy?

3. In the last section of the chapter, several movements and people who have shaped our contemporary understanding of fasting were described. Which ones have you been influenced by, and why? Are there other influences that you have experienced but are not described here? Which of these movements or individuals are the least familiar or comfortable to you, and why?

FOR PRAYER

If you had a strong reaction to any parts of this overview of fasting in

Christian history, pray about those reactions. Pray about the viewpoints that have influenced your understanding of fasting, asking God to speak his truth to you.

5

A PHOTO ALBUM OF
BIBLICAL STORIES

While they were worshiping the Lord and fasting,

the Holy Spirit said, "Set apart for me Barnabas

and Saul for the work to which I have called them."

Then after fasting and praying they laid their hands

on them and sent them off.

ACTS 13:2-3

Throughout Scripture fasting is assumed to be a normal part of the life of faith. It is described over and over in both the Old and New Testaments as a natural response in times of crisis, mourning or deep need. Jesus says "when you fast" (Mt 6:17), not "if you fast" or "perhaps you may want to fast."

The words *fast* and *fasting* are used about seventy-five times in the Bible. Approximately two-thirds of those occurrences are in the Old Testament and one-third in the New Testament. In addition, several fasts are described without using the word *fast*. In the Bible we find almost two dozen stories of people or groups of people who fasted. These passages offer insight into the purposes of fasting and the ways God answered prayers while people fasted.

While the Bible does provide multiple models for fasting, it does not give many specific instructions. The prophets talk about fasts that please and don't please God, and Jesus gives some very brief instructions. However, nowhere are we told how often to fast, what to fast from or how long to fast. Those of us who like to have concrete instructions will probably find the biblical passages frustratingly incomplete.

I suggest that you approach this chapter like a photo album. We'll look at more than a dozen snapshots of fasting from the Old Testament and a handful from the New Testament. Each page of the photo album—with several snapshots on it—will focus on a theme for fasting, such as mourning, repentance or asking God for help. Some of the photos are pictures of individuals, and others show communities fasting together. We'll look at people of deep faith, heroes and heroines who can teach us by their example.

After we look at these snapshots, we'll consider the words of instruction from the prophets and other biblical writers. Let's see what we can learn from the pictures God has given us in his Scriptures.

MOURNING

In the Old Testament, fasting and mourning are linked. Both express sadness before God. People wore clothes made of sackcloth (a rough, black cloth) and put ashes on their faces when they mourned, and they did the same when they fasted. Some of the earliest incidents of fasting express mourning. Our first page in the photo album has five photos of people who fasted when they mourned, three of them fairly early in Old Testament history and two of them quite a bit later.

After Saul's death. Saul, the first king of Israel, died in battle along with his three sons. A group of men rescued the bodies from the battle scene, brought them home and burned the bodies. These men buried the bones, then fasted for seven days (1 Sam 31:13). Like so many statements in the Bible about fasting, this snapshot simply shows that the men fasted. The passage does not mention why they felt fasting was an appropriate response, and we don't know what they didn't eat or didn't drink.

David and his friends. Our second snapshot follows the same pattern. Fasting is described as the response of David and his men at the news of Saul's death, with no reasons or specific details. David, who would be the next king, had been a close friend of Saul's son Jonathan. When David heard about the death of Saul and his sons, David tore his clothes, and all his men did the same. "They mourned and wept, and fasted until evening for Saul and for his son Jonathan, and for the army of the LORD and for the house of Israel, because they had fallen by the sword" (2 Sam 1:12).

Abner's death. In the early years of David's reign, Abner, a cousin of King Saul, volunteered to solicit support for David as king. He was treacherously slain by David's nephew Joab. When David heard about the death, he told all the people with him to tear their clothes, put on sackcloth and mourn over Abner. After the burial the people tried to persuade David to eat something, but David was determined not to eat until the sun set (2 Sam 3:35).

Esther. Jumping ahead to the fifth century before Christ, we meet Esther, a Jewish woman who became one of the queens of a Persian king in the city of Susa. An official in the court hated the Jewish people and encouraged the king to pass a decree to have all the Jews killed. When the decree was announced throughout the country, "there was great mourning among the Jews, with fasting and weeping and lamenting, and most of them lay in sackcloth and ashes" (Esther 4:3).

Nehemiah. Later Nehemiah served as a high official for the king of Persia. He got news from Jerusalem that the walls were broken down. He recounts, "When I heard these words I sat down and wept, and mourned for days, fasting and praying before the God of heaven" (Neh 1:4).

In all of these snapshots, something awful had happened, and fasting seems to have been an immediate and natural response, expressing grief and sadness. When we are deeply absorbed in grief, habitual activities and normal pleasures feel inappropriate and out of place. We want to shout, "Stop the world! The one I loved is no longer alive, and I can't bear it!" That desire to stop everything normal, to let ourselves be absorbed by our loss and pain, is manifested by stopping our consumption of food. Fasting while mourning can enable us to pray to God in our grief.

REPENTANCE

On the second page of our photo album, people in the snapshots continue to feel grief and sadness, but in these cases the sadness is related to personal sinfulness and the desire to repent before God. The yearly Day of Atonement, Yom Kippur, indicates God's establishment of the connection between fasting and repentance.

Yom Kippur, the Day of Atonement. Early in Israel's history, soon after Moses received the Ten Commandments, the yearly Day of Atonement was established. The people were commanded to stop working and to practice self-denial in the form of fasting and abstaining from all forms of pleasure for the entire day, twenty-four hours, from sunset to sunset.

Numbers 29:8-11 describes the special offerings of animals and grains that are appropriate for the Day of Atonement. Leviticus 16:30 gives the reason for this special day: "On this day atonement shall be made for you, to cleanse you; from all your sins you shall be clean before the LORD." God established one day each year for the people of Israel to remember their sins and repent by fasting and making offerings. Jewish people today still observe Yom Kippur with fasting.

Samuel. Our second snapshot linking fasting and repentance comes at the very end of the time of the Judges, the eleventh century before Christ. The prophet Samuel called the people of Israel to put away foreign gods, direct their hearts to the Lord and serve him only. The Israelites were threatened by the Philistines, a neighboring tribe, and Samuel believed the threat was caused by the people's unfaithfulness to God.

Samuel asked the people to gather at Mizpah so he could pray for them. The people put away their foreign gods and gathered together. They fasted that day, and said, 'We have sinned against the LORD'" (1 Sam 7:6). When the Philistines heard about the gathering, they drew near to attack. Samuel prayed for the people, and the Philistines were defeated.

Ahab. In the ninth century before Christ, Jezebel, queen of the Northern Kingdom, had a man killed in order to get a plot of land he owned. The prophet Elijah came to King Ahab to condemn this act. Elijah said God would bring disaster on Ahab's house because of this offense. When Ahab heard what his wife had done, he tore his clothes, put on sackcloth and fasted. God's word came to Elijah: "Have you seen how Ahab has humbled himself before me? Because he has humbled himself before me, I will not bring the disaster in his days; but in his son's days I will bring the disaster on his house" (1 Kings 21:29).

Jonah. God called Jonah to travel to the wicked foreign city of Ninevah to ask the inhabitants to repent of their evil. Jonah's attempts to run away from God's call took him into the belly of a fish for three days. Presumably Jonah

> *Pride and a too-full stomach are old bed-fellows. . . . Fasting, then, is a divine corrective to the pride of the human heart. It is a discipline of the body with a tendency to humble the soul.*

ARTHUR WALLIS,
GOD'S CHOSEN FAST

didn't eat while inside the great fish, but it would be hard to call that a fast because he had no choice in the matter. When Jonah finally did enter Ninevah and preach the need for repentance, he was totally incredulous that the people did repent. "The people of Ninevah believed God; they proclaimed a fast, and everyone, great and small, put on sackcloth" (Jon 3:5).

Nehemiah. In the fifth century before Christ, the king of Persia asked Nehemiah to return to Jerusalem to serve as governor of the fledgling colony of people returning from exile. Soon after their arrival, the people were read God's law, and they determined to keep it. First they observed a festival and feasted for a week, then they "assembled with fasting and in sackcloth, and with earth on their heads. Then those of Israelite descent . . . stood and confessed their sins and the iniquities of their ancestors" (Neh 9:1-2). Then they read from the law, made further confessions and worshiped the Lord.

These five snapshots show the connection between fasting and coming before God in sadness for sin. In the same way that fasting seemed to be a natural response when mourning, fasting seems to flow naturally out of repentance and a deep sorrow for sin. Fasting in these instances is a part of asking God for forgiveness. Our next group of snapshots continues in the theme of asking God for something. In these next seven photos, people fasted as they asked God for answers to a variety of kinds of prayers.

SEEKING ANSWERS TO PRAYER

Guidance. During the time of the Judges, a conflict arose between the majority of the tribes of the Israelites and one particular tribe, the Benjaminites. The conflict escalated into war, and after the second day of fighting, eighteen thousand Israelites lay dead. The soldiers who remained retreated to Bethel and spent the rest of the day weeping, fasting and making burnt offerings to the Lord.

As they fasted, wept and made offerings, the Israelites "inquired of the LORD," asking whether they should go back into battle the next day. God answered them clearly, telling them to go back into battle and saying they would prevail, which is precisely what happened (Judg 20:24-48).

Pleading with God. David, Israel's second king, used his power in a destructive way. He was attracted to Bathsheba, the wife of one of his military commanders. When the army was away at war, David stayed behind in Jerusalem and committed adultery with Bathsheba, and she became pregnant. To hide the adultery, David first tried to get her husband to come home and sleep with his wife. When that plot didn't work, David arranged for Bathsheba's husband to be killed in battle by putting him on the front line. David then married Bathsheba, and she gave birth to a son.

God confronted David with his sin through the words of the prophet Nathan, who told David that the child conceived in adultery would die. First the child became ill. "David therefore pleaded with God for the child; David fasted, and went in and lay all night on the ground" (2 Sam 12:16). When the child died on the seventh day, David's servants were afraid to tell him.

David could see the servants whispering together, so he asked if the child had died. When they said yes, David rose from the ground, cleaned himself up and asked for food. The servants were baffled. Evidently they were used to fasting as an expression of mourning, so they couldn't understand why David would start eating just after the child died.

David responded by saying, "While the child was still alive, I fasted

> *Fasting clears the mind and puts us in a posture of relinquishment. We give in to God better.*
>
>
>
> JAN JOHNSON,
> *FASTING AND SIMPLICITY*

and wept; for I said, 'Who knows? The LORD may be gracious to me and the child may live.' But now he is dead; why should I fast? Can I bring him back again?" (2 Sam 12:22-23).

When afraid. In the ninth century before Christ, Jehoshaphat was king in Judah in the south. Two neighboring nations, the Moabites and the Ammonites, were coming against Judah for battle. "Jehoshaphat was afraid; he set himself to seek the LORD, and proclaimed a fast throughout all Judah. Judah assembled to seek help from the LORD; from all the towns of Judah they came to seek the LORD" (2 Chron 20:3-4).

Jehoshaphat prayed eloquently before the assembly, asking God to remember his promises to his people. The prophet Jahaziel received a word from God saying that God would win the battle for them. Jehoshaphat and all the people fell down before the Lord in worship. The next day the army of Judah won the battle.

How long? The book of Daniel is set in the sixth century before Christ, when the people of Israel were in exile in Babylon. Daniel, a Jew, served in the court of two Babylonian kings. Daniel studied the prophet Jeremiah to try to figure out how long the exile would last. As he studied, he turned to the Lord "to seek an answer by prayer and supplication with fasting and sackcloth and ashes" (Dan 9:3). In a long and eloquent prayer, Daniel confesses the sins of the people of Israel and asks God for mercy for the exiles. In this snapshot, we see Daniel fasting both to repent of sin and to seek an answer from God.

Protection. In an incident similar to the snapshot of Nehemiah, Ezra, a Jew, was commissioned by the king of Persia to return with a group of exiles to his ancestral home in Israel and bring order there. Ezra had worshiped the God of Israel while living in Persia, and he expressed to the king his confidence that God would protect the Israelites on the journey. Because of his confidence in God, he was ashamed to ask the king for soldiers to protect them on the journey.

As the group began their journey, Ezra proclaimed a fast, "that we might deny ourselves before our God, to seek from him a safe journey for ourselves, our children, and all our possessions. . . . So we fasted and petitioned our God for this, and he listened to our entreaty" (Ezra 8:21-23).

Great need. When Esther and her uncle heard about the decree that all the Jews in Persia would be killed, they knew that Esther would have to intercede with the king on behalf of her people. Before she went to the king, Esther told her uncle, "Go, gather all the Jews to be found in Susa, and hold a fast on my behalf, and neither eat nor drink for three days, night or day. I and my maids will also fast as you do" (Esther 4:16). God answered the prayers of the Jewish people and spared them, a dramatic act of salvation that is celebrated by Jewish people every year during the festival of Purim.

Healing an epileptic boy. Fasting is linked to prayer in an incident when Jesus casts a demon out of an epileptic boy whom the disciples are unable to heal. After Jesus heals him, the disciples ask why they failed. Jesus responds, "This kind goeth not out but by prayer and fasting" (Mt 17:21 KJV; see also Mk 9:29). Most modern translations omit *fasting* but add a footnote mentioning it. Appendix B at the end of this book discusses why the translations differ on these verses.

In these seven snapshots, we see different prayer needs that motivated people to fast. Many of them were intense or even desperate needs. In most of these situations, the people had nowhere to turn for help except to God. We know very little of their motivation to fast. Did they believe God would hear their prayers more easily if they fasted? Did they think they needed to show God they were serious about their request? Were they desperate, and fasting just felt natural in the midst of their desperation? We cannot fully answer these questions, but we do know that throughout the Bible fasting was intricately linked with intercessory prayer. These pictures illustrate many different ways the prayer-fasting connection can look.

WORSHIPING AND HONORING GOD

In the Bible fasting seems to express a seriousness and intent to honor God, to give our lives to God alone. In these next snapshots, we will see the connection between fasting and worshiping God with our whole lives.

Daniel. While exiled in Babylon and living in the king's court, Daniel "resolved that he would not defile himself with the royal rations of food and wine" (Dan 1:8). So he asked the palace master to let him eat vegetables and water. The palace master was afraid that if Daniel did not eat enough he would look weakened, which would anger the king. Daniel talked the palace master's guard into trying a ten-day test for Daniel and his three friends. The guard agreed.

The result of the test? "At the end of ten days it was observed that they appeared better and fatter than all the young men who had been eating the royal rations" (Dan 1:15). So the guard continued to let Daniel and his friends eat vegetables, and God gave the young men knowledge, skill and wisdom. For these young men, staying away from the king's rich food served as a significant symbol of their dedication to the God of Israel.

Anna. The first fasting story in the New Testament involves the prophetess Anna, an eighty-four-year-old widow who "never left the temple but worshiped there with fasting and prayer night and day" (Lk 2:37). When Mary and Joseph brought the baby Jesus to the temple to be presented to the Lord, Anna was one of the first to recognize Jesus as the child who would bring about the redemption of Israel.

The early church. Some time after Jesus' death and resurrection, the Christians at Antioch were worshiping the Lord and fasting together. While they were praying, the Holy Spirit spoke clearly to them, telling them to set apart Barnabas and Saul for the work to which God was calling them. So the group of disciples laid their hands on Barnabas and Saul and sent them off (Acts 13:2-3). This incident illustrates that fasting was a normal and accepted part of the prayer practices of the early church. God spoke to the disciples while they were worshiping and fasting in a way that they may not have been expecting.

Entrusting leaders to the Lord. A short while later, Paul and Barnabas traveled through what is now Turkey and Syria, proclaiming the gospel and founding communities of believers. In each new church, they appointed elders, and "with prayer and fasting they entrusted them to the Lord" (Acts 14:23). As with so many of these snapshots, we don't know what motivated these early believers to fast as they prayed. We simply observe how fasting mattered enough to early Christians that they did it and recorded it in the book of Acts.

These four pictures portray diverse worship settings: Daniel desiring to keep himself pure in the pagan culture he lived in, Anna dedicating herself to worshiping God in the temple, the early Christians hearing God's guidance for Paul and Barnabas while fasting in community and prayer and fasting to set apart congregational leaders. As we move to the next three snapshots, the forty-day fasts of Moses, Elijah and Jesus, we will continue to see worship, dedication and experience of God's presence.

FORTY DAYS AND FORTY NIGHTS

Moses. In the very first fasting incident in the Bible, Moses goes up Mount Sinai to receive the Ten Commandments. In Deuteronomy 9:9, he remembers what happened: "When I went up the mountain to receive the stone tablets, the tablets of the covenant that the LORD made with you, I remained on the mountain forty days and forty nights; I neither ate bread nor drank water." Exodus 34:28 affirms that Moses was "there with the LORD forty days and forty nights."

This snapshot is the hardest to apply to our own lives because, without a miracle, no one can go forty days without water and live. We can understand Moses' supernatural fast by picturing him in God's presence on holy ground for those forty days, almost as if he were in heaven with God. Our bodily needs will be different in heaven, and we get a glimpse of that reality in this story. Moses' fast is a foretaste of the powerful reality expressed by the apostle Paul: "The kingdom of God is not food and drink but righteousness and peace and joy in the Holy Spirit" (Rom 14:17).

Elijah. In the ninth century before Christ, God called the prophet Elijah to confront the evil brought into Israel by Queen Jezebel's worship of foreign gods. One of the greatest confrontations occurred on Mount Carmel, where Elijah and the priests of Jezebel's gods erected two altars, set up sacrifices and called on their respective deities to bring fire to the altars.

The God of Israel brought fire to the altar Elijah had prepared and the sacrifice was consumed, while the priests of the false gods got no response. After this confrontation, Elijah was exhausted. Jezebel had threatened to take his life, so he fled into the wilderness. After a night there, the angel of the Lord brought Elijah food and commanded him to journey to Mount Horeb, another name for the mountain where Moses received the Ten Commandments. "He got up, and ate and drank; then he went in the strength of that food forty days and forty nights to Horeb the mount of God" (1 Kings 19:8). Both Jews and Christians have interpreted these words to mean that he fasted from food during his forty-day journey.

Jesus. Right after Jesus was baptized, the Spirit led him into the wilderness, where he fasted for forty days and forty nights. "He ate nothing at all during those days" (Lk 4:2). Satan came and tempted Jesus in three areas, and Jesus responded with statements from God's Word. After the temptation Jesus was "filled with the power of the Spirit" (Lk 4:14) and went to Galilee to began his ministry.

Jesus' fast and temptation established a foundation for his three years of ministry. In his weakest state, brought on by fasting, he was able to resist Satan's lures to gain physical sustenance, power and glory through his own strength rather than relying on God. His weakness from fasting and his reliance on Scripture demonstrated his utter and absolute trust in God.

These three fasts of Moses, Elijah and Jesus have shaped the church's understanding of fasting for two thousand years. Lent lasts forty days, and Lent has involved fasting in one form or another for most of Christian history. The supernatural aspect of these three fasts has encouraged believers to embrace fasting as a way to experience God's supernatural power and presence—for better and for worse. For example, people who shouldn't fast from food at all, such as those with medical conditions or eating disorders, sometimes read these stories and come to the dangerous conclusion that they should do something similar. On the other hand, many people have experienced significant spiritual growth through forty-day fasts from food and from other forms of gratification.

WORDS OF TEACHING

In our photo album we've seen a variety of people who fasted: Moses, Elijah, David, Esther, Jesus and many others. We've seen diverse reasons to fast: to mourn, repent, ask God for guidance or protection or help, or to plead with God to change his mind. We've seen individuals fasting, and we've seen groups of people fasting together. Now we will consider biblical passages that contain words of teaching about fasting.

A passage in the Psalms brings encouragement to people today who fast from all food and experience weakness. The psalm writer says, "My knees are weak through fasting" (Ps 109:24). How nice for us to know that people more than two thousand years ago felt frail and limp when they fasted from food, just as we do.

Two psalms show the connection in Old Testament times between fasting and wearing sackcloth:

> I humbled my soul with fasting . . .
> I made sackcloth my clothing. (Ps 69:10-11)

> I wore sackcloth;
> I afflicted myself with fasting.
> I prayed with head bowed on my bosom,
> as though I grieved for a friend or a brother. (Ps 35:13-14)

These two passages also show the connection between fasting and humble prayer.

We saw that when King David heard about Abner's death, he asked all the people to tear their clothes. Wearing torn clothes, like wearing sackcloth, was a sign of mourning. The prophets were concerned about the temptation for people to use signs of mourning—sackcloth or torn clothes—without having their hearts in the right place. The prophet Joel proclaimed God's word to the people:

> Return to me with all your heart,
> with fasting, with weeping, and with mourning;
> rend your hearts and not your clothing. (Joel 2:12-13)

Joel's words indicate that the central point of fasting is to turn our hearts toward God, not to focus on external signs of spiritual commitment like wearing particular clothes.

The prophet Isaiah recounts an argument between the Israelite people and God. The people ask:

> Why do we fast, but you do not see?
> Why humble ourselves, but you do not notice?

God's reply is stark:

> Look, you serve your own interest on your fast day,
> and oppress all your workers.
> Look, you fast only to quarrel and to fight

and to strike with a wicked fist.

Such fasting as you do today

    will not make your voice heard on high. (Is 58:3-4)

Isaiah states a truth that Jesus later emphasizes further. Fasting does not honor God when it is coupled with selfishness, pride or violence.

God's words through the prophet Isaiah put a whole new slant on fasting. Isaiah goes on:

Is not this the fast that I choose:

    to loose the bonds of injustice,

    to undo the thongs of the yoke,

to let the oppressed go free,

    and to break every yoke?

Is it not to share your bread with the hungry,

    and bring the homeless poor into your house;

when you see the naked, to cover them,

    and not to hide yourself from your own kin?

Then your light shall break forth like the dawn,

    and your healing shall spring up quickly. (Is 58:6-8)

The kind of fasting described by Isaiah—a way to share one's bread with the hungry—didn't catch on in ancient Israel or in New Testament times. We have seen that in the second century, Christians began to understand fasting as a way to free up funds for the poor. The roots of that practice came from these words of Isaiah.

"WHEN YOU FAST"

By the time Jesus came on the scene, fasting was well established as a Jewish discipline. The Day of Atonement was observed every fall with fasting. Four other fast days were observed over the course of the year (Zech 8:19). Faithful and observant Jews fasted twice a week, on Mondays and Thursdays, always wearing sackcloth and ashes on their faces as visible signs of their faithfulness.

Jesus talks about fasting in two settings early in his ministry. The first is in the Sermon on the Mount: "Whenever you fast, do not look dismal, like the hypocrites, for they disfigure their faces so as to show others that they are fasting. Truly I tell you, they have received their reward. But when you fast, put oil on your head and wash your face, so that your fasting may be seen not by others but by your Father who is in secret; and your Father who sees in secret will reward you" (Mt 6:16-18).

> *Fasting has every bit as much to do with the attitude of the heart as it does to what is actually given up in the fast.*

ANNA, A MUSICIAN IN HER THIRTIES

When Jesus says that the hypocrites "disfigure their faces," he is referring to the ashes people put on their faces as a sign they were fasting. People in Jesus' time put oil on their hair to look dressed up, so Jesus was suggesting that we do what we can to look normal and content when we fast. His words about fasting built on the words of Joel:

> Return to me with all your heart,
> with fasting, with weeping, and with mourning;
> rend your hearts and not your clothing. (Joel 2:12-13)

Fasting is about the inner attitude of our hearts toward God; it does not center on the way we appear to others or what others think of us.

The second time Jesus talks about fasting, he is responding to the questions of people who were comparing Jesus' disciples to other people of faith, specifically the Pharisees and the disciples of John the Baptist. "Why do John's disciples and the disciples of the Pharisees fast, but your disciples do not fast?" they ask. Jesus replies: "The wedding guests cannot fast

Fasting is a physical expression of heart-hunger for the coming of Jesus. . . . Jesus connects Christian fasting with our longing for the return of the Bridegroom.

JOHN PIPER,
*A HUNGER FOR GOD:
DESIRING GOD THROUGH
FASTING AND PRAYER*

while the bridegroom is with them, can they? As long as they have the bridegroom with them, they cannot fast. The days will come when the bridegroom is taken away from them, and then they will fast on that day" (Mk 2:18-20; see also Mt 9:14-15; Lk 5:33-35).

Christians throughout the ages have disputed the application of this passage to daily life. Was Jesus, the Bridegroom, "taken away from us" because he ascended into heaven (Acts 1:9), and therefore we should fast? Or is Jesus with us through the Holy Spirit (Jn 14:16-18), and therefore fasting is inappropriate? Most scholars have decided that despite the presence of God through the Holy Spirit, Jesus meant we should fast in the time between his first and second coming as an expression of our longing for his return.

BAD MOTIVES

Let's return briefly to our photo album, which would not be complete without a page picturing the misuse of fasting. Three biblical incidents show us that even good things can be abused.

Jezebel. In the ninth century before Christ, Jezebel was queen of the Northern Kingdom. She wanted a particular plot of land, a prime vineyard owned by Naboth, who was not interested in selling. Jezebel proclaimed a public fast, gathered the people together and sat Naboth at the head of the assembly. Then she had him killed and arranged to take his land (1 Kings 21:9-10).

The practice of fasting for selfish gain or manipulation of others is contemptible to God. The story doesn't end there, however. Elijah came to King Ahab to condemn this act, and Ahab ended up repenting and fasting, as we saw earlier.

The tax collector. Jesus told a story about two men who went to the temple to pray. The first man stood by himself and prayed, "God, I thank you that I am not like other people: thieves, rogues, adulterers, or even like this tax collector. I fast twice a week; I give a tenth of all my income." The tax collector prayed, "God, be merciful to me, a sinner!" Jesus told his disciples that the tax collector went home justified before God, not the first man, because "all who exalt themselves will be humbled, but all who humble themselves will be exalted" (Lk 18:9-14). After telling this story, Jesus emphasized that the attitude of the heart matters most. The practices of fasting or tithing, without the humility of a heart turned toward God, are meaningless.

The attempted murder of Paul. After the apostle Paul had significant success in preaching the gospel, he returned to Jerusalem. The Jewish leaders were determined to kill him, and forty of them bound themselves with an oath to fast until they succeeded (Acts 23:12). Paul's sister heard about the plot to ambush him, and he arranged to get away.

Two of these snapshots connect fasting to the intent to kill someone, and one of them involves self-righteousness manifested in fasting. As we have seen in the words of the prophets and of Jesus, fasting is not something that is good in itself; even fasting can be used for evil purposes. What matters is that we examine our motives for fasting to make sure we are truly seeking God's purposes and not our own.

LESSONS FROM SCRIPTURE

After looking at numerous snapshots and some general teaching, what else can we say for sure about the Bible's view of fasting? We have noticed that many different individuals fasted: kings and queens and ordinary people. The whole nation of Israel fasted one day a year, and the nation gathered to fast and pray for specific needs. The early Christians fasted. The incidents of fasting recorded in the Bible span its entire history, so we can see that the practice wasn't limited to one particular time or place.

Stories about fasting in the Bible receive very little commentary. Did David fast for the right reasons when his pleaded for the life of the child born to Bathsheba? Are the forty-day fasts of Moses, Elijah and Jesus just extraordinary events, or are they models for Christians today? What foods would the prophets or Jesus recommend that we omit when we fast? These are questions for which we have no definite answers.

However, we do know that in most instances fasting in the Bible was connected to prayer. Fasting expressed a variety of prayer concerns, ranging from mourning, repentance and sadness to prayers for particular needs and requests for God's guidance. Fasting was also connected to worship and submission to God.

The prophets and Jesus talked about fasting in a way that indicates it was a practice common enough to require some comments and guidance. Jesus says "when you fast," implying that fasting is an accepted and expected manifestation of faith in God. Jesus' words about the Bridegroom being taken from us are challenging and compelling. Yes, we have Jesus with us through the Spirit, but we also feel the loss Jesus' absence on earth creates in us. All Christians live in the tension of having the kingdom of God with us yet wanting more. Fasting is connected to our sadness at Jesus' absence and our desire for more of his presence.

Nowhere does the Bible command that we fast. We cannot say that fasting is mandatory or required as an expression of Christian faith. Still, fasting with prayer does express something significant, something that has been valued and practiced by Jews and Christians in many different places for millennia.

Richard Foster refers to the book *The Holy Exercise of a True Fast* by Thomas Cartwright, published in 1580, which discusses Jesus' teaching in the Sermon on the Mount (Mt 6:16-18). Cartwright points out that

Jesus' teaching about fasting stands firmly in the context of giving and praying. Foster comments, "It is as if there is an almost unconscious assumption that giving, praying, and fasting are all part of Christian devotion. We have no more reason to exclude fasting from the teaching than we do giving or praying." However, Foster emphasizes that these words of Jesus do not constitute a command.

"Sanctify a fast, call a solemn assembly," says the prophet Joel. "Gather the elders and all the inhabitants of the land to the house of the LORD your God, and cry out to the LORD" (Joel 1:14). We still cry out to the Lord. Fasting deepens and intensifies our cries.

QUESTIONS FOR REFLECTION, JOURNALING AND DISCUSSION

1. Which of the fasting themes in this chapter are the most attractive to you? Which are the most challenging? Which feel threatening or inspire fear?

2. When you consider our photo album as a whole, do you agree that the Bible seems to take fasting for granted? Why or why not?

3. What did you learn from the pages of this photo album? What did you learn from the words of Jesus and the Old Testament prophets about fasting? What seems most relevant for you today?

FOR PRAYER

Pick two or three of the snapshots from this chapter and look them up in your Bible. Read them carefully and then pray through them. Ask God to help you discern the way these stories might apply to your life. Ask God to teach you truths from his Word that still apply today.

6

ABSTAINING FROM FOOD

Jesus said to them, "The wedding guests cannot fast
while the bridegroom is with them, can they?
As long as they have the bridegroom with them,
they cannot fast. The days will come
when the bridegroom is taken away from them,
and then they will fast on that day."

MARK 2:19-20

I had eaten no rich food,
no meat or wine had entered my mouth.

DANIEL 10:3

Nicole reflects, "When I fast, it changes everything. It's like the air is
different."

Nicole, a teacher, and her husband, Ed, a businessman, fast from food
in several ways. During Lent each of them gives up a particular food.

Nicole usually chooses sugar, one of her favorite foods, and Ed often fasts from chips, which he loves. In addition, when a problem or need seems "huge," they will fast from all food for a day in order to devote more time to prayer, together and alone, about that issue. During those one-day fasts, Nicole will drink only water. Ed has found that when he engages in a water fast, he has a hard time working. So on their fast days, Ed drinks juices.

For Nicole, fasting from food—whether a water fast or a fast from just one kind of food—is "a pulled apart space, a sacred space. I try to pray about the fast beforehand to see what God would have me do. In order for it to work for me, I have to define all the edges of it, the beginning and the end, and determine exactly what I will consume and not consume."

Fasting helps Nicole pray more often and more deeply, but she tries to resist one idea that can creep into her thoughts. "Fasting is as much about listening to God in prayer as it is about asking God for something. I'm not comfortable with turning it into me giving up something big for God, so then God is obligated to answer my prayers."

Nicole and Ed have three children, in middle school and high school. During their one-day fasts, Nicole continues to prepare meals for their children, who understand that their parents are fasting. The children are not obligated to join in. During Lent the children are invited to fast from one food, but Nicole and Ed offer them the freedom to participate or not.

Nicole's and Ed's fasts fit into a long-standing pattern among Christians. Throughout most of Christian history and in most religions of the world, the word *fast* relates to refraining voluntarily from eating food for a season and for a spiritual purpose. In this chapter we will look at several forms of food fasts, and we will consider some of the practicalities, challenges and motivations of each form. Because of our consumer culture, however, I am advocating a view of fasting that also includes refraining from things other than food. We will explore options for media, shopping and entertainment fasts in chapter seven.

SOME VOCABULARY OF FASTING

- Water fast—refraining from eating all solid food, drinking only water
- Juice fast—refraining from eating all solid food, but drinking fruit or vegetable juices or clear broth
- Partial fast—refraining from eating one food or a group of goods; includes Daniel fasts, Eastern Orthodox fasts and many Lenten fasts
- Daniel fast—eating only vegetables
- Eastern Orthodox fast—refraining from eating all meat, fish, dairy, eggs, oil and alcohol
- Complete fast—refraining from consuming all food and liquids for a very short time. Many experts on fasting recommend avoiding complete fasts.

Over the centuries Christians have fasted from food in three major ways:

- Partial fasts, which involve abstaining from one or more kinds of food
- Water or juice fasts, which involve refraining from all solid food
- Complete fasts, in which no food or liquids are consumed

PARTIAL FASTS

Anyone who has given up chocolate, coffee, potato chips or alcohol for Lent has participated in a partial fast. Seldom do we use the word *fast* to describe Lenten discipline, but the word is appropriate.

"I love sugar, so I often give up candy for Lent," says Gina, a software consultant in her forties. "When I find myself reaching for candy, it calls me to remember that Christ gave himself for my sins, sacrificed himself for me. When I do this little sacrifice, I am reminded of his much bigger sacrifice. I enjoy having a reminder during Lent that helps bring Jesus to my mind more frequently than usual."

Gina's motivation—experiencing her sacrifice as a memory device to connect in a small way with Jesus' sacrifice—is common in partial fasts. Another common motivation is the desire to break the power of a food that has become addictive. A third motivation is to simplify eating patterns for the sake of discipline and to identify with the poor. All of these motivations lead to a deeper connection to Christ.

"I've been influenced by the Eastern Orthodox approach to fasting," says Neal, a Protestant minister in his fifties. "Like Eastern Orthodox Christians, I prepare for feast days like Christmas, Easter and Pentecost by eating more simply. I limit my portions, and as much as possible I eliminate meat, fish, eggs, dairy, oils and alcohol. This is a way to draw closer to the Lord and to discipline our bodies for God's glory. It is an attempt to simplify our lives so we can stand against the indulgence of the flesh that is so common in our culture. This is a big challenge because 'feasting' goes on year-round, nonstop in our Protestant churches."

Eastern Orthodox Christians remember that in the Garden of Eden, Adam and Eve ate only fruits and vegetables. Fasting in this tradition comes from a desire to remember paradise and regain its purity. In Eastern Orthodox churches no one fasts alone; the whole community fasts, and adaptations are provided for children and pregnant women. Such community support makes a big difference in fasting because no one brings rich cookies over to another person's house on fast days, and at church events on fast days people bring appropriate foods. People can share with each other their struggles and their recipes. At the end of the fast, everyone feasts together as well.

Bread and vegetables have always been the food of the poor—the simplest and least expensive food available. When we voluntarily agree to share this food, we become more tangibly connected to the poverty of millions who struggle to put food on their plates.

AMY JOHNSON FRYKHOLM,
"SOUL FOOD,"
CHRISTIAN CENTURY

The Old Testament prophet Daniel ate only vegetables and drank only water because of his powerful desire to steer clear of the rich food and wine served in the king's courts. A "Daniel fast" is even more simplified than the Eastern Orthodox fasts, and some people have adopted this form of fasting as a way of living counterculturally, like Daniel did. In Africa a Daniel fast means only one meal a day of fruits and vegetables.

Many monks and Christian leaders of past centuries engaged in partial fasts. They consumed only bread and water at one meal or for a day, a week or even longer.

Olivia and Carlos, both in their early thirties, recently fasted from foods that need to be cooked. They began their fast the evening before Good Friday and continued until Easter morning. They made an exception for their one-year-old son, Drew, using the microwave to heat up his food. Olivia describes their motivation: "It's traditional in some Christian circles not to light a fire—the stove was our version of fire—on these days as a way of entering into the cold darkness of the tomb with Christ. I had made a lot of cold salads and breads earlier in the week that we fed off of for those two days, so it was a small thing, really. But I tell you, our Easter morning tea and toast never tasted so good!" In addition, Olivia noticed the gift of time from not having to cook. "It freed up a lot of time to play with Drew, to read and pray, to stare out the window. It was wonderful."

Any of these varieties of partial fasts are excellent places to get started with fasting. Partial fasts remind us of Christ's sacrifice and thus help us draw closer to the Lord. Partial fasts help us unhook from our culture's oft-repeated message that if we want something, we should get it right away. A partial fast is an excellent way to prepare for a feast because the rich and abundant food of a celebratory meal will taste richer if we have simplified our diet ahead of time.

Partial fasts nurture thankfulness, as we experience going without something we normally take for granted. Even small efforts to simplify our diets for a season can help us connect with the poor of the world. We may take for granted that sweets, meat or dairy products are on our table every day. When we do without them, we more easily remember the large number of people around the world who don't have enough to eat day after day.

I want to emphasize that some people need to eat every day: children, pregnant and nursing women, diabetics and others with medical conditions. Some people are on medications that must be taken with food. These people can participate in a partial fast and still reap many of fasting's benefits.

Some people who have had a troubled relationship with food—those who have dieted a lot or engaged in compulsive eating—may find that partial fasts enable them to participate in a way that makes space for God and does not trigger obsessive thoughts about food and weight. They need to start with very brief partial fasts and examine carefully whether it is helpful or harmful as a spiritual discipline in their lives. People who have experienced anorexia or bulimia should not engage in any kind of food fasts, including partial food fasts.

JUICE AND WATER FASTS

When we go without solid food entirely, we enter into a different kind of fast. Juice and water fasts change the chemistry of the body in a way that fosters spiritual awareness for many people. They talk about the intensity of their connection with God and the tender intimacy they experience. Juice and water fasts are much more physically demanding than partial fasts, and most experts suggest a consultation with a doctor before embracing a juice or water fast of longer than twenty-four hours.

WHO SHOULDN'T FAST FROM ALL FOOD

People who shouldn't engage in juice, water or complete fasts:

- Women who are pregnant or nursing
- Anyone who has an eating disorder or has had one in the past
- Children under twelve (teens should be supervised if fasting from all food)
- Diabetics and people with kidney disease
- The frail elderly
- People who must take medication with food
- People with a cold, the flu or some other temporary illness

People with a medical condition should check with their doctor before engaging in a fast from all food. People who have dieted a lot or engaged in compulsive eating should fast from food carefully, beginning with brief partial fasts, to see if this is a helpful or harmful spiritual discipline for them.

In the 1990s Bill Bright, the former president of Campus Crusade, was a strong advocate for forty-day juice fasts and encouraged many Christian leaders to participate. The length recalls the fasts of Moses, Elijah and Jesus, but a water or juice fast can be much shorter than forty days. If you want to engage in a juice or water fast, begin with fasting for a meal or a day, then work up slowly to longer fasts.

Andrew, an engineer in his thirties, fasts on Fridays during Lent. He skips one meal, usually lunch, and drinks plenty of water to avoid headaches. He reports, "The nagging hunger serves to center me on God while I'm at work, where it's easy to get caught up in thinking about only what I need to get done. This kind of fasting is an effort to expand a sense of God-mindedness beyond the sabbath."

Some people refrain from eating before Communion, originally a Catholic and Eastern Orthodox tradition that can be deeply meaningful. One man engaged in this practice with a friend. He remembers, "Our first nourishment of the day would be the Communion elements. I felt moved that there was nothing but Jesus in my stomach, just as I desire that there be nothing but Jesus in my life."

Richard, in his forties, works for a Christian nonprofit organization. He likes to fast from everything but water and his morning cup of coffee from sundown Sunday to sundown Monday every week. He describes his experience: "The most impressive thing for me about fasting is how unspiritual it has been. It almost always turns into a struggle to get through the last hours without eating. I often break my fasts before I intend to, but I am always impressed with the value of being in want. When I fast and think about people who live in constant want—lacking the love of God, health, food—I am humbled, because I bear up very poorly."

Craig, a minister in his fifties, also fasts one day each week. Craig has Mondays off, and he fasts every Tuesday as he begins his workweek. He skips breakfast and usually lunch, and he drinks lots of water. He reflects, "Fasting helps train my body and my mind that the lord of my will is not my physical nature, such as hunger pains, even if that nature is a part of how God made me. The Lord of my life is Jesus Christ. By learning to say no to the flesh, I learn to be more sensitive to saying yes to Jesus, whether in a time of fasting or not."

People report that during food fasts it feels like there are more hours in the day, which gives a different feel to the day and allows for intentional action in many areas, including prayer. Betsy, a mother and home-

Food is necessary to life, but we have made it more necessary than God. How often have we neglected to remember God's presence when we would never consider neglecting to eat? Fasting brings us face to face with how we put the material world ahead of its spiritual Source.

MARJORIE THOMPSON,
SOUL FEAST

maker in her forties, says, "I am a sort of hyperactive person, and what I've found with fasting is that even if I'm running around leading my normal ADD life, on a day that I fast, I keep getting hungry. Each time it happens it reminds me to pray, like a little prayer alarm clock going off periodically."

People who have experienced both long and short fasts from food usually report that the longer fasts are actually easier. The first three days are often the hardest. As we will see below, the body's chemistry changes around the third day of a fast from solid food, and that change has a profound impact on the way a fast feels.

"The first couple days of a juice fast are usually pretty painful, with hunger pangs, headaches and stomach cramps," Anna, a musician in her thirties, reports. "Once I reach the third day, something levels out; I get into the rhythm of the fast and I don't miss the food. I've reached the end of three-day, five-day, seven-day and twelve-day fasts feeling very sad that I will start eating again and will lose the experience of intimacy with the Lord that is tied to the fast. The Lord has always met me profoundly during times of fasting. I've noticed increased clarity in hearing the Lord, increased patience to wait on him and to listen, increased revelation from his Word or through dreams, and increased discernment."

For Anna, juice fasts foster intimacy with God. Some people experience that close connection, but others don't. We heard from Richard, who experiences water fasting as "unspiritual" but very humbling. We have different bodies and different responses to going without food.

THE PHYSIOLOGY OF FASTING FROM ALL SOLID FOOD

To understand what happens when we fast from solid food, we need to look at the biochemistry of withholding food. A juice fast supplies some calories, while a water fast supplies none. Let's first consider what happens when all calories are withdrawn.

Our organs, particularly our brain, heart and lungs, require continuous fuel. In the absence of fuel from food, the body draws on its stores of nutrients. The easiest stores to access are found in the liver and muscles. During the first day or two of a fast from all food, the liver and muscles release sugar and amino acids (protein building blocks). For most people it is safe to empty these stores of sugar and amino acids, but they will feel quite hungry. For diabetics and people with some other medical conditions, however, it is not safe.

The sugar in our liver holds up to several pounds of water. As the sugar is used up in the first few days, the stored water is released, so the scale will usually register a rapid weight loss of many pounds. This is mostly water and will return when food, particularly carbohydrates, is added to the diet again.

In the first few days the intestines empty out and bowel movements become very infrequent. A few experts recommend enemas to help the bowel empty itself, but most experts believe they are not necessary.

Most people have headaches during the first few days of a water fast if they are withdrawing from caffeine. Experts on fasting recommend eliminating caffeine gradually over the several weeks before the fast. Headaches can also be caused by insufficient water. A person fasting from all food should drink at least two quarts of water a day.

Toxins are also released from the body, causing unusual smells, fatigue and headaches. Drinking a lot of water will usually help reduce these symptoms.

After a day or two the sugar and amino-acid stores in the liver and muscles are used up. On the second or third day the body begins to use stored fat as fuel. This marks a significant change. The liver converts stored fat into ketones, which are used by the body in place of glucose, or blood sugar, our most common fuel.

When our bodies use ketones for fuel, we enter a state called *ketosis,* which is dangerous for diabetics (called *keto-acidosis* in that case) and people with kidney disease. For most healthy people ketosis is simply different, not dangerous. For many people ketosis definitely feels different because the brain is using a different fuel than normal.

Many people who have fasted testify that ketosis can be a state of heightened spiritual awareness that makes prayer easier and makes the spiritual realm seem more real. Ketosis has another benefit. The appetite is usually significantly reduced, which makes the fast much easier after two or three days have passed.

I have been in ketosis several times, and my experiences have varied. My appetite is much less intense, and I experience fewer food cravings. I usually feel somewhat lightheaded. One time I experienced significant ease in prayer that I still remember as deeply joyous. Heaven somehow seemed close to me, and I marveled at the ways I could see God's hand at work in the world. Unfortunately, that wonderful nearness of God has not been typical every time.

Many books on fasting report that as long as the body still has fat to burn, the appetite will continue to be suppressed; then when all the fat stores are gone, the appetite will return. People of average weight can fast for somewhere around forty days before the fat stores are gone and the appetite returns. The Gospel of Luke reports that when Jesus fasted in the wilderness, he was "famished" at the end of the forty days (Lk 4:2). Some people who have engaged in long fasts believe that after forty days without food and likely without much appetite, Jesus had probably used up his stored fat. He was probably experiencing intense hunger as a natural symptom of what was happening in his body. Satan's temptations likely would have been even more difficult for Jesus when ketosis had ended and his appetite had returned in full force.

Most people on a water fast feel weak and tired enough that they cannot work. Thus juice fasting has become popular because juice provides just enough calories to get many of the benefits of water fasting but with more energy.

In a long juice fast the body may or may not enter the state of ketosis, depending on the quantity and type of juices consumed. Most people experience a decrease in appetite after two or three days, indicating they have probably entered into a state of mild ketosis. Just like in a water fast, many may experience the spiritual benefits of ketosis. Prayer may become more natural, and the spiritual realm may feel more real.

Most experts recommend light exercise, such as walking, during juice and water fasts. More strenuous exercise is hard to do, particularly during water fasts. The rhythm of walking has the added benefit of aiding prayer.

Some experts recommend a combination fast, with several days spent consuming juices, several days with water only and then several more days of juice. This sends the body gradually into the deepest state of ketosis, providing a gentle entry into water fasting as well as a gentle exit.

In both juice and water fasting, particularly after reaching the state of ketosis, people feel cold. Summer is a great time for a long juice or water fast. In winter long underwear may be very helpful. Blood pressure usually drops, so the person may feel lightheaded. Ketosis causes a noticeable difference in the smell of the skin and particularly the breath. Some people experience an array of odd symptoms such as diarrhea or vomiting, rashes or even boils on the skin. Feeling cold and lightheaded and having a different smell are normal during a long fast, but other symptoms should be discussed with a doctor.

PREPARING FOR THE FAST

Experienced fasters talk about the significance of preparation. They ask, Does God indeed desire this fast? What might God want me to pray for? A significant increase in prayer time before the fast will help it to be effective in us drawing closer to God.

One of the ways fasting from food blesses us is that we can pray and study the Bible during the time we would normally spend shopping for, preparing and eating food. Before the fast spend some time considering what this will look like. If you are going to fast during breakfast in a busy household, how and where will you make time to be with the Lord? If you are going to fast during lunch at work, where will you go during your lunch break?

The temptation for many people is to use the extra time to work or do something mindless like read magazines or watch TV. How will you avoid that temptation? Can you put your Bible and prayer journal somewhere conspicuous so they are ready to use? Can you put the TV or your stack of magazines in a closet for the duration of the fast? Planning ahead can make a big difference in maintaining the Christ-centered focus of the fast.

In fasting I am reminded that God is my sustenance.

BETHANY, A DIETITIAN
IN HER TWENTIES

Some people find that juice or water fasts go better when they prepare by eating smaller meals and reducing the consumption of animal foods ahead of time. For most people, however, the significant preparation for a fast is spiritual, not physical.

ENDING A FAST

After a fast of any length, it is tempting to eat a steak dinner, spaghetti with meatballs or some heavy, favorite food. After missing only one or two meals, a big, rich plate of food may not have any repercussions. After a fast of several days or longer, it is extremely important to re-engage with food very slowly. After a long water fast, have some juice first. After a long juice fast, eat only small portions of food for several meals before returning to your regular diet. People who fast regularly have favorite foods to break the fast, such as fruit or light soups. Keep the servings small.

People who dive right into eating large quantities of rich foods may have very bad stomachaches. The first hours and days after a fast are a precious time of reflection on what God did during the fast. Losing that time to the pain of a stomachache will negate some of the benefit of the fast.

A youth group leader used to get several pizzas for the participants at the end of a Thirty Hour Famine. It was a big mistake, he remembers, because everyone felt sick after eating. His group members felt much better eating a light meal after the fast.

After a fast take some time to reenter life slowly. Perhaps the TV and magazines could stay in the closet for a few more days, allowing more time for prayer, reflection and reading the Bible. What did God do in your life during the fast? What did you learn? What are you more thankful for? What has God called you to repent of? What do you want to change in your life because of what you learned?

COMPLETE FASTS

The Old Testament describes many complete fasts, in which no food or liquids were consumed. Moses fasted from food and water for forty days on Mount Sinai (Ex 34:28). This required supernatural intervention because normally a person can live only a few days without water. Queen Esther and all the Jews in her land stopped eating food and drinking water for three days as they prayed fervently to God for deliverance (Esther 4:16). The apostle Paul did not eat or drink for three days after he saw Jesus on the road to Damascus (Acts 9:9).

In our time, Muslims engage in a complete fast during the daylight hours for the month of Ramadan. They are commanded to swallow nothing during daylight, including their own saliva. They can eat and drink during the night, and many Muslims enjoy the month of Ramadan because of the family intimacy experienced during the nights of feasting and the days of sacrifice.

Jews fast on Yom Kippur, the Day of Atonement, consuming no food or liquids. Several other fast days in the Jewish calendar also call for abstaining from all food and water for a day or part of a day.

Over the past two thousand years very few Christians have encouraged complete fasts. As we have seen, the Christian tradition has usually emphasized water fasts or partial fasts of bread and water, abstinence from meat or rich food, or Lenten disciplines of refraining from eating treats of various kinds. In the twentieth century juice fasts came into prominence because they allow participants to experience many of the benefits of water fasting without extreme fatigue.

There may be times when God will call an individual or community to engage in a complete fast—no food or liquid—for a short time. If you feel led to engage in one, be sure that God is guiding you in that direction, and be sure to do it only for a very short time.

WHY FAST FROM FOOD?

Fasting from food connects us in a primordial way with profound and significant truths. Food and water are essential to life. The sin of Adam and Eve involved food. The feasts and celebrations of key moments in salvation history involve food. Mealtimes with family and friends can be among the greatest gifts of life—times of hospitality, warmth and community. Food communicates blessing and abundance.

Food comes to us as a gift from God. Psalm 104 talks about the variety of animals God created along with humans. "These all look to you to give them their food in due season," the psalmist says (Ps 104:27).

Yet when Jesus was tempted by Satan he said, "One does not live by bread alone" (Lk 4:4). Jesus was quoting Deuteronomy 8:3, which discusses the time the Israelites wandered in the wilderness for forty years. God allowed the people of Israel to experience hunger in the wilderness "in order to make you understand that one does not live by bread alone, but by every word that comes from the mouth of the LORD."

God's work in our world and God's Word in our lives are infinitely more significant than food. By voluntarily stepping into hunger, we affirm that truth. When we fast, we suspend our participation in one of the great joys of life—eating—in order to engage with a greater joy—God.

When you are fasting and you feel hungry, you are to remember that you are really hungry for God.

LAUREN WINNER,
MUDHOUSE SABBATH

QUESTIONS FOR REFLECTION, JOURNALING AND DISCUSSION

1. What forms of fasting from food might be appropriate for you? Are juice and water fasts unhealthy for you because of medical issues, a past or present eating disorder or a history of compulsive eating or dieting? If you cannot engage in a juice or water fast for these or other reasons, can you see yourself engaging in a partial fast of some sort? Or would you be better off engaging in fasts that do not involve food? Is there someone you could ask to help you explore the kinds of fasting that might work for you?

2. What does food mean to you? What are the joys connected to food? In what ways do you experience community around food?

3. What experiences have you had with hunger, and what do they mean to you? What do you think it would mean to you to stop eating for a short time?

4. Is God calling you to fast from food? What are your motivations for
   fasting?

FOR PRAYER

Ask for God's guidance about whether you should fast from food. If you
have fasted before, ask for guidance about whether you should try a new
form of fasting from food. Ask others to pray with you for discernment
about this.

7

OTHER FASTS

"All things are lawful for me,"
but not all things are beneficial. "All things are
lawful for me," but I will not be dominated by anything.

1 CORINTHIANS 6:12

Meredith, a writer in her twenties, fasts when she notices something in her life that is not bad in itself, like TV or shopping, is becoming too high a priority. "I often desire a lot of stuff I don't need. When those things get in the way of stuff I really do need—like strong relationships, thinking time, long walks, prayer time, meditation and self-reflection—I cut out those things I don't need for a season so they can regain the proper place in my life."

Laurie's motivations are similar. Laurie, a minister in her forties, has fasted from restaurants, solitaire on the computer and the kinds of fiction she perceives as "mindless." She says, "All these fasts are about breaking dependencies. They are great tools for nurturing mindfulness of God's presence, intentionality and creativity in the daily routines of life."

Fasting removes a layer of self- and society-inflicted smog so that the truth appears more clearly.

MEREDITH, A WRITER IN
HER TWENTIES

Kristen, in her twenties, has fasted from favorite hobbies and music, "anything that has become an idol in my life." She says that one of the first results is having a lot more free time. But, she says, "more importantly these times of abstinence have helped me to reevaluate my priorities and refocus my attention on the Lord."

In the past, the word *fasting* was reserved for giving up some or all foods for a period of time. But as we have seen, Christians today use the word *fast* to describe abstinence from a variety of things for a season and for a spiritual purpose.

THE MODEL OF 1 CORINTHIANS

The apostle Paul's first letter to the Christians at Corinth can help us understand this way to fast. In his letter Paul answers a number of questions the Corinthians had sent him. Some of those questions concerned sex. Is it more spiritual, the Corinthians wondered, for a married couple to live together without engaging in sexual intercourse? Paul answered with a resounding *no*. It is much better in general, he said, for couples to be sexually intimate so they won't be tempted into sexual sin.

Paul does say, however, that a couple can choose to refrain from sexual intimacy by mutual agreement "for a set time, to devote yourselves to prayer" (1 Cor 7:5). Paul doesn't use the word *fast,* but this is a pattern that can inform our engagement in fasting from things other than food. In fact, some couples today do fast from sexual intimacy for a set time, for the purpose of prayer.

Sex is normal and good in a marriage relationship. Yet sometimes we set aside things that are normal and good in order to focus more intensely on prayer for a time. Sometimes we notice that aspects of our daily lives have become too important. In the past they may have been healthy and life-giving, like sexual intimacy in marriage, but now for some reason they have grabbed ahold of us. They have assumed a place out of proportion to their true meaning and value. So we set them aside for a season to pray. As we pray, we often learn how to restore balance to our lives and how to keep God at the center. Sometimes we will make permanent changes in our lives because of what we experience during such a fast.

Sometimes God calls us to set something aside even when it is fruitful and seems good in just about every way. Yet by setting aside that practice or activity, we make space for something new from God.

In 1 Corinthians Paul is advocating the intentional setting aside of something good in order to embrace something better. It is only for a season, however. We are not hyperspiritual people who are supposed to embrace extreme self-discipline all the time. In fact, extreme self-discipline can become an idol in itself.

In this chapter we will hear numerous stories from people who have fasted from a variety of things for a variety of reasons. Before we hear these stories, let's look briefly at the forces at work in our culture that make these forms of fasting appropriate today.

"MORE, MORE"

We are surrounded by voices. The voice of our culture comes to us in advertisements on TV and radio, in magazines and newspapers, on billboards and even in bathroom stalls. We hear the priorities of our culture as we watch TV shows and movies, as we read novels and magazines, and as we play video games and visit websites. Our culture's voice clamors in just about every place imaginable.

The cacophonous prattle seems random and unfocused, drawing our attention to a mishmash of objects like cosmetic surgery and hardware tools and financial management software. Underlying all the scattered topics, however, are only a few themes. More is better. Focus on what you don't have, and do whatever it takes to get it. Get more money, more beauty, more sex and more power. Focus on getting more because more is always better.

Can we hunger for Christ, the Bread of Life, when we are full of dishes enticingly served up on the steam table of a prosperous consumer culture? From what do we need to fast today so we may develop strength of soul tomorrow?

JOHN S. MOGABGAB,
WEAVINGS JOURNAL

The good news is that God speaks continuously also. "The heavens are telling the glory of God. . . . Day to day pours forth speech" (Ps 19:1-2). God's voice speaks of abundance and joy, release from slavery through Jesus Christ, power through the Holy Spirit, comfort in sorrow and peace in the midst of trouble. God's voice calls us to use our gifts to be the hands and feet of Jesus in our hurting world. What can we do to hear God's voice more consistently and tune out the voices of the culture more easily? What can we do to reclaim the freedom that God intends for us?

Fasting is one of many spiritual disciplines that helps us hear God's voice in place of our culture's cacophony. Fasting enables us to step outside all the noise. By choosing to have less of something for a season, we are more able to put things into perspective, to affirm with Jesus, "Is not life more than food, and the body more than clothing?" (Mt 6:25). We are more able to "strive first for the kingdom of God and his righteousness" (Mt 6:33) so that food, clothing and other things we need can be received from God as gifts, and we are no longer consumed by them.

MAKING SPACE FOR GOD

Sometimes fasting simply makes space for aspects of our spiritual life that need a boost. Bethany, a dietitian in her twenties, enjoyed fasting one year during Lent from the music she usually listens to. In its place she chose twenty-one Christian songs that she felt helped to center her focus on God. For her, those six weeks with those particular songs helped her worship God afresh.

Another woman, in her fifties, has a tendency to "numb out" with mystery novels and movies. From time to time she chooses to fast from novels and movies for the purpose of challenging and feeding her brain with Christian truth. She usually feels called to fast when she's a part of a Bible study and is getting behind in her preparation for it.

Debbie, a mother of three in her thirties, gets headaches when she fasts from food, so she no longer engages in water or juice fasts. Debbie asked herself the question, "Why fast?" That question helped her begin the practice of fasting from information for one to three days at a time. In her life, sources of information include TV, radio and the Internet.

Debbie's answer to her own question was to devote more time to prayer, which led her to consider how to meet that goal. She remembers that when she used to fast from food, she always felt there were more hours in the day. Those hours were a gift, and she was determined to use that gift for prayer and contemplation. "Now," she says, "when I fast from information it is with the same intent. The quiet of the house with no TV and no radio, the quiet of the car, the absence of distractions speak to my heart, and I find it easier to pray."

Debbie warns that fasting is an act of personal devotion. It is not public. "Jesus' warnings about fasting still apply today. It is not to be a sign of a holier-than-thou living."

BY MYSELF BUT NOT ALONE

Corinne, a Weight Watchers instructor in her early fifties, engaged in a fast that made space in an unusual way for a new experience of God. Corinne is a very social and outgoing person with a wide network of friendships. She talks with people, even strangers, very comfortably about the Christian faith and about God's work in her life. She often prays with friends. In fact, Corinne experiences God's presence most often in relationships with others.

Corinne has low blood sugar and does not engage in water or juice fasts. She does fast during Lent from certain foods she enjoys. However, her most meaningful fast came recently when she trained for an athletic competition—alone. Corinne has frequently participated in marathons and triathlons, always in the company of friends. She enjoys helping inexperienced athletes prepare for these big events.

Recently Corinne and her family moved to a new neighborhood. Soon after the move, it was time to begin her three-month training to run the Seattle half marathon. Normally Corinne would round up a group of friends, including some inexperienced runners, to train together at one of Seattle's parks. Instead, God seemed to be leading Corinne to train by herself by running in her new neighborhood. This was the first time she had ever attempted to train on her own. Early in the season as she was praying while running, she heard the words, "By myself but not alone."

Corinne got to know the roads and neighborhoods around her new house, which helped her feel a part of her new community. God was present in her times of running alone in a way she had never experienced before. Because of her theme words, "By myself but not alone," as she fasted from training with other people she was expectant of God's presence in a new way.

Corinne's family and friends, who know how much she likes to be connected to people, cheered her on during her "By myself but not alone" project. Now that Corinne is back to training with friends, she finds she is less likely to sense God's presence with her as she runs. The total fast from training with others was somehow a key for her to experience God's presence in a new way. She is praying about whether to do it again.

LONG-TERM TRANSFORMATION

A fast can help us get out of a rut that has ceased to be life-giving. Sometimes a fast results in a permanent change. Sometimes habits change, and sometimes an inner attitude changes.

"My newspaper fast was a Lenten exercise," says Lina, a teacher in her forties. A few years ago she substituted the Bible for her morning newspaper during Lent. She found she liked it so much that she continued the practice. "I continue to read the paper later in the day if I have time, but starting the day with Bible reading instead of the newspaper has, as you can imagine, made a huge impact on my outlook, my faith and my understanding of who God is in the world and in my life."

Olivia, the mother of a one-year-old son, has fasted in a variety of ways during Lent. One year she fasted from TV. She remembers being addicted to a soap opera. She had been recording it during the day and watching it at night with her roommates, a habit she wanted to break. She reflects on that Lent: "The six weeks without TV were hard sometimes, but not watching TV freed up a lot of time for reading, walking and praying. That was probably one of my most fruitful Lents."

After Lent, even though her roommates were still watching the soap opera every night, Olivia didn't go back to it, which she perceives to be a gift of grace from God. Eventually she lost interest in TV, and when she got married, she and her husband decided to be TV-free. That was five years ago, and she is still grateful for her Lenten TV fast that got her started on a journey that has continued to bear fruit.

Audrey, a nursing student, decided to fast from makeup during Lent of her freshman year of college. "I realized I had started to dislike my appearance without makeup, and I was starting to care way too much about whether or not guys noticed my appearance. So I chose to put

When I began reading the newspaper after a newspaper fast, the freshness of it made me very aware of advertising and the cynicism in so many of the comics.

GRETCHEN, A HOMEMAKER
IN HER FORTIES

away makeup for Lent and allow God to redefine my perception of beauty. It is so easy as a girl living in a college dorm to get caught up in the comparison game of insecurity, wondering how one measures up to the rest of the crowd. My generation has such a distorted picture of what authentic beauty is, and I didn't want to get caught up in that."

During that Lent Audrey tried to let God teach her what he considers to be authentic beauty. "That fast broke up a minor stronghold in my life. I haven't depended on makeup ever since. I still wear it sometimes, but now I care a lot more about the authentic beauty of holiness." Audrey's habits changed, and her inner attitude changed as well.

For Teresa, the mother of six-year-old twins, Lenten fasts from newspapers and TV news have made her more aware of her habits all year long. Teresa calls herself a "news junkie." Often for Lent she gives up newspaper reading and TV watching during the day, saving it until her girls are in bed. These newspaper and TV fasts have convicted her of her own sin in three ways.

First, she has come to realize that when she's watching TV or reading the newspaper, she isn't as available or interactive with her family. Second, she has identified "the sin of squandering time, of not even being aware of how much time has gone by, lost forever, on pursuits that largely do nothing to glorify God or help anyone else or bear fruit in me."

Third, she realized that newspapers and TV news nurture anxiety in her. "I began to see that reading every horror story about a disaster befalling some child or every detail of the next terror alerts was contributing to my own anxiety, which has been a besetting sin for me. I have wept over things I read in the paper or saw on the news, thinking that God would be pleased that I am identifying with the suffering of others. There is some truth in that, and sometimes it leads me to pray for the people involved. But more often it creates in me a spirit of heaviness that I carry around in a low-key, background-noise kind of way. My husband has helped me see that I need to be more aware of the effect the things I put into my heart and mind have on me."

Teresa's Lenten discipline has helped during other times of the year to limit her exposure to media. "I don't consistently do this—sometimes I enjoy the time to read the whole paper—but I am more aware, even during the times that I'm not fasting, of the choices I'm making when I spend time that way."

BREAKING A COMPULSION

God may call us to engage in a fast that breaks the power of a habit in our lives. "I can develop a compulsion to read the newspaper," says Larry, a campus minister in his sixties. "At times I stop my subscription. And I would do the same with TV if I observed that it had a hold on me."

You met Lina, a teacher in her forties, a few pages ago. One year she fasted from shopping during Lent. She reflects, "The fast from shopping—other than grocery shopping—happened at a time when I found myself very focused on buying clothing for myself. The fast from shopping broke the hold that particular form of materialism had on me at the time. I really felt much more able to focus on

Fasting teaches us to be sweet and strong when we don't get what we want.

DALLAS WILLARD

God's priorities." During her fast she stayed out of stores, but the biggest challenge would come when a catalog arrived in the mail. She learned she needed to put catalogs in the recycle bin as soon as they arrived.

Lina's shopping fast occurred several years ago before Internet shopping became so common. A shopping fast today would have to address that challenge as well.

SOMETHING NEW FROM GOD

Sometimes God calls us to fast from something that appears to be a good and healthy part of our lives so we can experience new things in its place. In Anna's case, God called her to fast from something that was central to the way she serves others in Christ's name.

Anna, in her thirties, plays the guitar in her congregation's praise band. She often plays her guitar and leads the singing for retreats and conferences. For relaxation, she plays the guitar and sings praise music with her friends and when she's alone. Imagine her surprise when she felt God leading her to fast from her guitar for a season. As she began the fast, she thought it would last only for Lent. Instead, God called her to continue it for a whole year.

Anna declined all invitations to lead music at retreats and conferences. She took a break from the praise band. Her decision was not popular, and she felt beat down by the criticism of her fellow musicians and members of the congregation, who enjoyed her music leadership so much and didn't want her to stop.

For Anna, the guitar fast exposed the things that fed her emotional health. "I like people to be happy. I don't want to

> *In a more tangible, visceral way than any other spiritual discipline, fasting reveals our excessive attachments and the assumptions that lie behind them.*

MARJORIE THOMPSON,
SOUL FEAST

disappoint people. I like to serve and meet needs." And yet God called her to stop that form of service. As the weeks of her guitar fast went by, she felt she had lost a major part of her identity.

Anna wondered how in the world she was supposed to worship, when worship for her had always included praise music that she played on the guitar. She found a bitter spirit within herself when she attended worship services. She would come into the sanctuary, sit down and look at the bulletin and begin to criticize. Why did they choose these songs? Why are they singing them in this order? How can I worship during a song I don't like?

She began to hear God speaking to her. God seemed to be saying, "If you can't worship me for who I am, then we have a problem." She realized that worship had become centered around her needs: What am I going to get out of this? She stopped looking at the bulletin and told herself she didn't come to church to criticize. She was there to worship God, and that's what she began to do in a new way.

She learned that her intense engagement with music during corporate and private worship had closed her eyes to other aspects of worship, particularly intercession. During that year of her guitar fast, Anna's engagement with intercession blossomed. She joined several intercessory prayer groups and found great joy in fasting and praying for needs around the world.

Anna's guitar fast ended a couple of years ago, but her engagement in intercessory prayer has not. God used the guitar fast to open Anna to something new, a significant part of her ongoing ministry.

HEARING GOD

In this chapter we've seen a variety of different patterns of fasting from things other than food. Sometimes we are called to fast from something for a season simply to make space for God. Sometimes God calls us to fast so that there will be space for something new. Sometimes God uses a fast to transform our habits or our attitudes permanently. All of these results are rooted in the prayer that takes place before, during and after the fast.

When we fast, we step outside our normal habits. Those habits may be good ones—such as eating, keeping up on the news, relaxing with a good novel—but we set them aside to pray. Sometimes in fasts we set aside habits that have come to have too much power in our lives, such as excessive TV watching that has engulfed more important things. We hope that the fast will help us put that habit back in balance.

Fasting is not a way to deal with sinful behavior such as gossiping, slandering our workmates or adultery. God calls us to forsake such practices every day, not just for a set time during a fast. When a habit involves a life-damaging addiction, we need to take serious action such as medical treatment or participation in Alcoholics Anonymous or other support groups. The central purpose of Christian fasting is to clear away daily pleasures so we can approach God in new ways. Fasting is not medical treatment or a temporary cure for sinfulness.

In a culture gone mad with calls for more consumption, fasting from entertainment, media or shopping is a countercultural act. Fasting denies the message that all needs and wants should be met immediately. Fasting from things other than food helps us affirm in an experiential way that our relationship with God matters more than possessions or self-focused recreational experiences.

However, fasting isn't a way to prove that we can deny ourselves. People who fast frequently talk about the fact that God is the one who calls us to fast, and God must direct our fast. Fasting is a part of a relationship, a part of an ongoing conversation with God. God calls us into a fast. We respond in obedience. God partners with us in the fast, guiding us, speaking to us through the Bible, strengthening us and enabling us to pray more frequently and more powerfully. Ultimately we hope that God will transform us, giving us a deeper heart for intimacy with him.

How might we hear God's voice calling us to fast? Sometimes a Scripture passage will come alive. Sometimes we will hear something—in a sermon, from a friend, in a Bible class—that nudges us toward a particular fast. Sometimes a growing conviction in our hearts, a kind of inner voice, urges us to fast. Sometimes in prayer or reflection we become aware of a growing imbalance in our lives. At times we long for a deeper experience of God, and fasting seems like the best way to respond to that longing.

One woman began a TV fast because of a dream. In her dream she walked past her TV. On the TV was a Post-it note with the words, "Choose today whom you will serve." She had been noticing that her TV was always on, filling every moment with sound and images, and she had been wondering if God might be calling her to take some action. The dream confirmed her feeling that perhaps she should fast from TV for a season.

Arthur Wallis's classic book from forty years ago is titled *God's Chosen Fast*. He writes about abstaining from food, but his words apply to other fasts as well. He strongly believes that it is God who appoints our fasts. Wallis advises, "If you have been brought low through personal defeat; if there is a call in your soul to a deeper purifying, to a renewed consecration; if there is the challenge of some new task for which you feel ill-equipped—then it is time to enquire of God whether He would not have you separate yourself unto Him in fasting."

> *Fasting, like prayer, must be God-initiated and God-ordained if it is to be effective.*
>
>
>
> ARTHUR WALLIS,
> *GOD'S CHOSEN FAST*

Wallis's words make clear that we can initiate a dialog with God, asking if fasting is the best way to approach a particular need. We need to wait for God's answer. Perhaps this is not the time to fast, for reasons that might become clear much later. Perhaps an addictive behavior needs to be dealt with in a different way. But perhaps fasting is just the right way at this time to deal with a need or a problem or a longing. God will direct us.

QUESTIONS FOR REFLECTION, JOURNALING AND DISCUSSION

1. As you read this chapter, did you feel a pull toward a certain kind of fasting? Describe the pull or longing you felt.

2. If the purpose of fasting is to make space for prayer, what might you fast from that would create that time and space? Make a list of possibilities and consider the pros and cons of each one.

3. Is there something in your life that is overused or in danger of becoming an addiction? Something taking up time or energy that might go to other things?

4. How does God usually direct you? Through an inner nudging? Through the Bible? Through the words of friends or sermons? How might you make space to hear God's voice on the best ways for you to fast?

FOR PRAYER

Pray about the patterns of how you use your time. Ask God to show you the practices and habits of your life that you could cease from for a season in order to pray more.

8

FASTING IN COMMUNITY

Jehoshaphat was afraid; he set himself to seek the LORD,
and proclaimed a fast throughout all Judah.
Judah assembled to seek help from the LORD;
from all the towns of Judah they came to seek the LORD.

2 CHRONICLES 20:3-4

Charlotte, a retired teacher in her seventies, fasted with others from all food several times for three days as part of a class at church. She remembers, "Those were times of heightened awareness of my dependence on God and on my church community. There was a sense of sharing that was an important part of the experience. I wish my community would encourage us to do it together again."

Emily, a mom in her fifties, participated in three forty-day juice fasts as part of a nationwide Youth With A Mission emphasis on praying for the spread of the gospel. She knew that people around the country were fasting at the same time, using the same list of specific prayer requests related to world evangelization and the needs of the church around the world. She remembers the joy of "being part of a big movement, part of something bigger."

COMMUNAL FASTING IN THE BIBLE AND AROUND THE WORLD

Slightly more than half of the fasting snapshots in the Bible involve groups of people fasting together. Some people fasted both alone and in community. King David fasted alone to pray that his baby son wouldn't die. He also fasted with his friends and colleagues when Saul and Jonathan died, then again when Abner died. Daniel fasted alone when he was seeking an answer from God about how long the exile would last, and he fasted with his friends when they decided together not to eat the rich food of the king's court.

In other stories we see strong models for community fasting in order to pray together with power. King Jehoshaphat gathered all Judah together to fast and pray for God's help in battle. The Ninevites fasted together to repent. Ezra fasted with his fellow travelers to pray for God's protection. Esther fasted for three days with her servants and all the Jews of her city. Jews throughout history have fasted together on the Day of Atonement.

Jesus' words about fasting in secret seem to indicate that we should fast alone so no one else knows we're fasting. Yet in Acts we have two stories about Paul and Barnabas and local church leaders fasting and praying together. Many Christians throughout history and around the world today have interpreted Jesus' words to mean that we must not flaunt the practice of fasting. We must not fast to impress people. The motive of our fasting matters—to draw near to God—and we can do that in community or alone.

Christians in North America and other Western countries have much to learn from the Christians in Africa, Asia, and Central and South America. Fasting is an integral part of the Christian life in many parts of the world. My husband visited Kenya recently and attended a large, thriving church where dozens of new Christians were baptized the Sunday he was there. He was surprised to find that the church bulletin gave the dates of congregational fast days for that month, along with prayer requests to be addressed during the fast. The fast days were listed with other dates of the congregation's events for that month. Fasting in that church is an accepted, normal, everyday part of congregational life.

Trent, a missionary in Asia, remembers the first time he engaged in a long fast, lasting approximately two and a half weeks. His purpose was to pray for direction for his ministry's future in light of the change of government in Hong Kong in 1997. Toward the end of the fast Trent was in China to meet with the leaders of a major house-church network. Their meeting of ten or twelve people involved a big meal. When someone asked Trent why he wasn't eating, he said he was fasting and explained why. His Chinese host responded, "You should have told us, and we would have all fasted with you." Trent reflects, "I can't imagine that kind of response in the United States, where fasting is such a personal thing, not common or corporate."

Fasting in community has a long history, going back more than three thousand years. Fasting with a friend, a spouse, a small group, a class, a congregation or a community of congregations gives a sense of richness and companionship to the fast, an experience of being a "part of something bigger." Fasting is much easier when we know that others are partnering with us at the same time. Fasting with others mutes some of the negative voices we may hear inside us when we fast because we can rest in the fact that others are moving ahead with confidence.

People who fast together can also feast together afterward, making the experience rich and full. In this chapter we will look at multiple models for fasting with others. We will also consider the impact on children when their parents fast.

WITH ONE OR TWO PARTNERS

Sara was recently divorced. When she first began to realize her marriage was falling apart, she told two close friends and asked for their prayers. The two friends suggested they all fast from food one day a week to pray for Sara's marriage. Sara was grateful for their support and joined in the fast days with them, praying fervently for guidance for her marriage. The weekly fast days lasted for several months.

Now, after the divorce is an unfortunate fact, Sara remembers those communal fast days with warmth and gratitude. She felt loved by her two friends and supported by their care. She also felt empowered in her prayers on that one day each week.

The simplest way to fast with others is to fast with one or two partners, as Sara did. The partners could include a spouse, a relative, a friend or someone from church. The benefits begin long before the fast starts. You can discuss your plans for the fast with your partners, including what to fast from, how long it will last and what it will look like to feast afterward. You can also discuss your fears and concerns.

You can plan for the ways you will support each other during the fast. Will you phone or email each other regularly? Will you meet and talk about how the fast is going? Will you meet and pray with each other? You can talk ahead of time about the ways you hope to grow in prayer and agree to pray for each other as you seek to listen to God. As you fast and pray, you can talk about the ways God is shaping your prayers in new directions by the guidance of his Spirit.

You and your partner or partners can fast from different things, and you can even fast at slightly different times. Don't forget the time after the fast. Debrief together shortly after the fast ends, then be sure to talk again several weeks later. You will probably find that you continue to process your experiences for several weeks.

IN A SMALL GROUP

The same principles for fasting with one or two partners can be expanded to fasting with a small group. Nicole and Juliet are members of a women's Bible study and prayer group. About two years ago one of the group members was facing a major decision, and several other members of the group had significant prayer concerns. The group decided to engage in a juice fast beginning after dinner one day and ending before dinner the next day in order to pray for these needs. They felt strongly that they wanted to fast on the same day.

Nicole had fasted many times before, alone and with her husband. For her, this fast with her small group was a bonding and intimate time. As they evaluated the fast afterward, Nicole could see that it had nurtured the connection between the women and built up their faith.

Juliet had never fasted before. She was very anxious and made a determined plan to sing praise songs whenever she felt weak or hungry. On the day of the fast she had two major commitments that differed from her normal daily schedule. Juliet remembers: "I took a fast from my entire usual routine and created a special day for myself, which felt like part indulgence and part worship. I'm glad I did it—it gave me a chance for new perspective on my routine and the elements of my day that I didn't think I could easily do without. At the end of the fast, I was amazed at how terrific I felt—cleansed, focused, relaxed, almost euphoric—was it the flush of achievement or God's grace? I don't know."

Fasting with a group provided an excellent introduction to fasting for Juliet: "I definitely felt more inspired and supported knowing that we were all committed to fasting, that the others thought it was doable and that we would share the experience on the same day. I also felt accountable to our plan. There was no way I was going to postpone fasting on that day just because it seemed inconvenient. I thought of my comrades throughout the day and felt glad I could spend part of the day with one of them. I really enjoyed that bond. When we discussed our experience afterward, we all gained more perspective by comparing notes. The shared experience definitely brought us together as a group."

ROUND-ROBIN FASTING

Nicole and Juliet's group fasted on the same day so they could experience a sense of community by doing the same thing at the same time. Another pattern of group fasting involves taking turns so that someone is fasting and praying every day for a particular need.

Carol, a pastor, frequently organizes people in her congregation to fast and pray one day a week for people who are ill. Recently she did the same thing in her extended family. She observes, "Something about both fasting and praying makes our response seem more tangible and active, particularly when people are feeling helpless in the face of a difficult diagnosis. My own family is clearly divided on a number of faith issues. Organizing them in round-robin fasting and prayer when my sister was diagnosed with a brain tumor was a great experience that brought us unity. Her tumor turned out to be a rare cyst, correctly diagnosed by the third doctor in the providential series of events. She is now recovering with great prognosis for better health than she has had in years."

Somehow fasting adds emphasis to my prayers, as if it is my way of saying, "Okay, God, I'm serious about this one."

NATALIE, A PROJECT MANAGER IN HER TWENTIES

Round-robin fasting is also called chain fasting. Some churches, particularly overseas, ask people to sign up to pray and fast once a week for particular projects and needs. The chain fast may last for a month, several months or a year.

IN A CONGREGATION

Sylvia is a pastor's wife in Colombia, South America. In her congregation fasting is a very important part of the life of the church. Thursday is their regular fast day. The congregation fasts for a week at the beginning of each year to seek the Lord's direction for the year ahead. They also have congregational fasts, usually lasting a week, during the year as the Lord leads.

Everyone in Sylvia's church is encouraged to participate in whatever way they can. Most people engage in a juice or water fast, but others— such as those who work strenuous jobs or those with health issues— may fast for only one meal a day or may eliminate certain foods. Children are encouraged to eat lighter for one meal, perhaps eating only fruit, or to fast from television on the weekly fast day. Sylvia says, "We are not strict about how the person fasts, but we do ask them to participate in some way, perhaps cutting out heavier foods. Each one is to know from the Lord what he is to do."

During the weeklong fasts, prayer meetings are held every evening. One year a weeklong fast in October went so well and the prayer times felt so rich that the congregation decided to continue for a second week. One topic for prayer that week was the desire to start a school. They had no idea how to begin. Three days after the fast, they were invited to attend a conference on Christian education. The main speaker had planned a trip to Brazil but felt strongly led to visit Colombia as well. He made the decision to come to Colombia during the two weeks the congregation was fasting and praying. The school is now a major part of the congregation's ministry and is accredited by the government.

> *Each fast serves as a time of dedication to the Lord. I am making a statement, both to myself and to the Lord, that he matters to me and is well worth the sacrifice.*

ANNA, A MUSICIAN
IN HER THIRTIES

Sylvia notes, "People here take prayer and fasting seriously. Basically we are reminding ourselves that our own flesh and natural mind are not what rule our lives. Jesus is King. We are also telling the Lord that finding his will is important to us, more important than food." People in the congregation are sensitive to God's leading to set aside times of fasting to pray for personal needs as well. Sylvia says that at any given time at least one person in the congregation will be fasting because, she says, "It is a way of life to be able to hear better from the Lord."

THE OCTOBER FAST

A multiracial congregation in the Midwest of the United States has held an annual monthlong fast for more than ten years. They call it the October Fast. Each year the pastors and other congregational leaders choose a theme. Early in September the congregation's leaders begin to talk with the congregation about purposes for the fast. They create a booklet each week containing a Scripture focus as well as daily prayer requests for the church and the world.

Each week has a different focus, building toward more challenging forms of fasting from food. The first week the congregation is encouraged to fast from dinner; the second week, from breakfast and lunch. The third week they are encouraged to fast from meat, and the fourth week, to try a juice or water fast. The congregation is invited to give the money they save as a hunger offering, which benefits people who don't have enough to eat.

During the second through fourth weeks of the fast, everyone is also encouraged to engage in a fast from media, picking one kind to refrain from. This makes it possible for all congregation members to participate, even those unable to engage in juice and water fasts. Children are encouraged to participate by giving up a favorite food. Everyone is encouraged to use the time saved by fasting for prayer.

Jacqueline, a staff member at the church, reflects that the fast "brings the congregation together. People have prayer partners during the fast, and they make a plan for how often they are going to talk on the phone and pray together."

Jacqueline believes fasting is an important part of the Christian life because it addresses so many of our needs. "Fasting is for purification. It helps us hear God more clearly. Sometimes when we have a decision or choice that's hard to make, fasting enables us to hear God. Fasting also helps us identify sins in our lives that comfort covers.

"When we fast, we're not trying to impress God. This is not a performance with the goal of manipulating God. God is not a genie in a lamp that we can rub and ask for things. Fasting helps us get in a place where we can hear God."

Jacqueline acknowledges that congregational leaders have to do a lot of teaching about the October Fast because there is so much misunderstanding around fasting. Each of the weekly booklets prepared for the fast contains a basic introduction to fasting written by the pastor, explaining common pitfalls and misconceptions and giving positive reasons to fast.

As a Nation

Fasting is an integral part of the Christian life in many parts of Africa. The presidents of Kenya and Zambia have called for national days of fasting and prayer in times of crisis. Every year or two many of the churches and mission agencies of Uganda band together to call for forty days of fasting for the nation. Pastors from many churches meet for three days of prayer and fasting before they invite all the Christians of Uganda to join in. Christians are invited to pray in homes, schools, workplaces and neighborhoods for God's work in their nation. In addition to the forty-day fasts, Christian leaders often call for single days of prayer and fasting at various times during the year.

Leah, a Ugandan Christian, reports that most Christians in her country fast at least one day a week. They may fast from all food, drinking

Christians who fast say that it sharpens and sensitizes their spiritual faculties to become more in tune with what God is doing throughout the world.

BILL BRIGHT,
THE TRANSFORMING POWER OF FASTING AND PRAYER

fruit juice or water. They may engage in a "Daniel fast," eating only one meal on the fast day, a light meal of vegetables and fruit. Sometimes people engage in an "Esther fast," abstaining from both food and water for three days. Some people will do a "Jesus fast," fasting for forty days once or twice a year.

Christians in Africa and many other parts of the world have not absorbed the myth that is promoted so pervasively in the United States. They do not believe that God will make life easy. They do not believe that suffering is a sign that God has abandoned us. They understand that suffering shapes our character and that Christians should want to embrace voluntary suffering in the form of fasting because of the significant spiritual benefits.

Leah reflects on daily Christian life in Uganda: "There is a deep faith in God. Unlike the West, we are aware of the spiritual realm as a very real entity. People understand that things are first achieved in the Spirit before they are made manifest in the physical, therefore they strive to exercise their spiritual potential to the maximum in fasting and prayer. Even the focus of answers to prayer is perceived in the spiritual realm first rather than what is seen." Truly Christians in Western countries have much to learn from those in other parts of the world.

Leah says that Christians in Uganda see fasting combined with prayer as a significant means of Christian obedience and growth for individuals, congregations and the nation. Fasting helps Christians discern spiritual things more clearly and hear God's voice more often. It brings humility and greater power to prayers. It increases faith and often breaks the bondage of "besetting sins" and addictions. Some people experience healing from disease after a fast, particularly after a long one. Fasting nurtures a deeper longing for God's presence. Fasting and praying for the nation shape history in directions that are consistent with God's values.

PRAYER AND COMMUNAL FASTING

When fasting with a friend or small group, brainstorming prayer topics ahead of time can be very helpful. When fasting with a congregation or a larger community, the leaders of the fast often lay out prayer requests so everyone can be praying for the same needs. This partnership in prayer can be one of the great blessings of fasting in community.

Many people who fast regularly report that their prayers change over the course of the fast. Anna, who fasts frequently both from food and from things other than food, notes that she always starts a fast with specific prayer requests in mind. As the fast progresses and as she prays for those specific needs, new concerns come up, and she begins to pray for them. Often she ends a fast praying for something entirely different from the concerns she had at the beginning. Other times when the fast ends, she finds she is praying in a different way for the same needs she started with. These changes in prayer come from listening to God as she prays and reads the Bible.

The support of a community can be very helpful over the course of a fast as the direction of prayer changes. Having a partner or small group means having someone to talk with about the way God is guiding the prayers during the fast. Afterward, as prayers continue, the guidance received from God during the fast can help direct the way the group prays.

Fasting promotes dialogue with God. We listen for God to speak to us even while we speak our concerns and requests to God. We are wise if we talk over what we believe we are hearing from God with our Christian brothers and sisters, checking to see if they have heard God speak in a similar way. "Test the spirits to see whether they are from God," the apostle John recommends (1 Jn 4:1). When we believe we have heard God speak, we need to examine what we have heard by comparing it to the truth in the Bible and by discussing it in community. Fasting with others gives us that opportunity.

IN FAMILIES

Spouses who fast together have the opportunity to share struggles, prayer requests and the results of listening to God. Should children be included in this partnership in fasting? Children under twelve should not engage in fasts from all food because it could hinder their growth and development. But they can participate in fasting in a limited fashion, by giving up a favorite food or a favorite activity. Should they be encouraged to do that?

Nicole, the teacher and mother of three teenagers, has fasted in many different ways over the years. Before Lent, Nicole and her husband include their children in their conversations about fasting. "We invite them to find something to fast from, and they have done it some years and not others. Sometimes they are very creative." She remembers when one of her sons designed a different fast for every week of Lent: candy, TV, pop, videos and so on. The weekly variety helped him stay with it.

When Nicole fasts from all food, she tells her children the basics of what she's doing—not eating so she can pray more. "It always seemed like walking a fine line," she says, "not wanting to give too much attention to the fast and also not wanting to be too vague."

When Nicole's children were younger, she planned ahead carefully and prepared food ahead of time so she wouldn't have to do too much cooking while fasting. She tried to visualize the various food needs of her family and tried to anticipate ways to meet those needs ahead of time.

Alan fasted from all food one day a week for a year to pray for his daughter's special needs. He told his children that he was fasting, and he explained that he was using this time to pray. He didn't go into any more detail than that, and his children never asked what he was praying about. He sat with his family during dinner on his fast days and drank his water.

Vincent fasts when he wants to pray deeply about something. He drinks only water for a day, several days or a week, depending on the intensity of the prayer need. His children are now grown, but he remembers sitting with the family at the dinner table and drinking water. The children's curiosity seemed to be satisfied with a simple explanation about going without food to focus on a particular prayer concern. It was an accepted pattern to his children because they had always seen their father fast.

Vincent believes children learn more from what they see than from what they are told. He and his wife never tried to involve their children in a fast but simply assumed they would learn something about prayer from seeing their father fast. That indeed proved to be true. Vincent's daughter, now in her twenties, is a woman deeply committed to prayer. She fasts regularly.

Other parents affirm the same pattern. Children easily grasp the explanation that the parents aren't eating so they can focus on prayer. Children can be welcomed into the fasting community by being invited to give up something they value, such as a favorite food, a toy or a common activity in order to pray more. Family fasting should have a lightness about it, a true choice rather than forced participation, so children and teens can decide whether or not to participate in a fast.

Barbara, a social worker in her forties, has fasted from TV, shopping and movies. She tries to strike a balance between fasting as an example to her teenage daughters and encouraging them to participate with her. As children get older, fasting provides an opportunity to discuss the lures of our culture and the many forces that pull us away from God. Barbara says, "We try to fast as a family from things that use up our time without us thinking about it. Then we talk about how easy it is for those things to take up our time when they don't really bring value into our lives."

Fasting, with brief explanations to children and more detailed explanations to teens, can help shape family life, demonstrating that our faith in Christ is more important to us than our consumption of food, entertainment, media or clothes. Fasting in community can provide the support and encouragement necessary for perseverance and significant growth. Fasting as a congregation can shape the congregation's direction as well as influence the growth of individuals. Fasting as a nation can shape history.

QUESTIONS FOR REFLECTION, JOURNALING AND DISCUSSION

1. If you would like to try fasting or if you have fasted on your own in the past, brainstorm who might become a fasting partner with you. Is there an individual or a group of people with whom you could fast? What benefits might you experience by fasting in partnership or in community?

2. If you have children in the home, what concerns do you have about embracing fasting? How might you explain fasting to your children? How might you invite them to try fasting? What benefits might come to them because you fast?

FOR PRAYER

Pray about any desire you find in yourself to have a partner or a group of partners as you fast. Ask for God's discernment about how to move forward.

9

TODAY MORE THAN EVER

Worship the Lord your God, and serve only him.

JESUS, QUOTING DEUTERONOMY 6:13
(MATTHEW 4:10)

While I was writing this book, I decided to try some new ways of fasting. I'd gotten into my own little fasting rut: water fasts connected with weight loss, which did not have significant lasting spiritual impact (surprise, surprise); and my Lenten fast from colorful jewelry, which has been deeply meaningful but is, after all, only one way to fast. When I did the research for this book, I began to realize how many ways there are to fast and how few of them I had experienced.

In chapter one I described one of the simple fasts I undertook during the writing of this book. On a day that I needed to make four car trips, I fasted from music while driving so I could pray for a friend's need. I was pleased to find that the road noise—and the sound of my failing muffler—did indeed remind me to pray.

I also decided to try a fast from food every Friday during the writing of this book. I like Fridays as a fast day because of the connection to Jesus' death on Good Friday, a day of great sacrifice for a wonderful and life-giving purpose. As I prayed about how to fast on Fridays, I realized I wanted to try Eastern Orthodox fasting, refraining from eating meat, eggs, dairy and oil. I wondered if someone like me, who has struggled with weight almost all my life, could fast in that way as a gift to God and as a way to pray more deeply while staying untangled with issues of weight loss.

On Thursday of the first week, I began to think about what I might eat the next day. Breakfast was fairly easy because I often eat cooked oatmeal with fruit and without milk. Lunch and dinner were harder to plan.

Fasting is meant to awaken us to the hunger of the world, not just our own hunger.

JOHN PIPER,
A HUNGER FOR GOD: DESIRING GOD THROUGH FASTING AND PRAYER

I'm perfectly happy to eat masses of vegetables, as long as I can cook them in olive oil. I enjoy rice and beans and lentils, as long as I can cook them in chicken broth or sprinkle them with cheese when I serve them. Without animal products and without oil, how could I flavor the simple food I would cook?

As I planned for that first day of Eastern Orthodox fasting, I realized that the meals I eat are almost always flavored with the foods of affluence: meat, milk products or olive oil. I began to think about the people who cannot consume these expensive foods because of financial hardship. I was overcome with sadness for them and for the way I have taken for granted my own affluence.

In the past when I engaged in water fasts, I found myself praying for the very poor of the earth, those people who are hungry and lack enough calories to thrive. As I engaged in Eastern Orthodox fasting, I found myself thinking about and praying for people who have enough to eat but lack the luxury of variety that I experience every day of my life and that I take for granted so easily.

I found myself close to tears several times at my own arrogance and lack of gratitude. This deep repentance slowed me down and brought me into God's presence in a wonderful way. On my fast days I found that I read the newspaper in a different light, feeling more sympathy for people in all kinds of need.

The disadvantage of Eastern Orthodox fasting is that it doesn't necessarily free up more time for prayer, especially at first. I found I had to think harder about what foods to cook and eat. After a while I got used to fixing flavorful foods seasoned with fruit or curry, but cooking still took time. Later, as the food planning became easier, I realized this form of fasting is about simplicity, the freedom to step outside our customary habits, the freedom to set aside the rich foods we are used to and embrace the simplest forms of eating.

I did find that I prayed much more often on Fridays. Cooking and eating differently definitely reminded me to pray. On most of the Fridays, that increased prayer time came naturally, without hooking me into diet mode. However, on one Friday I didn't eat very much because I was just too lazy to cook. As I experienced hunger, I could feel myself beginning to wonder if I might lose weight that day. I prayed much less that day and instead thought about my weight. I realized that for fasting to work for me, a person who has dieted far too much and engaged in too much compulsive eating, it needs to be disconnected from feeling hungry.

One of the main reasons
I have chosen to fast is
because fasting sharpens
a person's sensitivity
to the Lord.

KRISTEN, IN HER TWENTIES

One Friday I woke up and simply forgot I was planning to fast that day. I had thought about it on Thursday, but I woke up hungry for eggs, so I fixed them for breakfast. It was midmorning before I remembered I had intended to fast from animal foods that day. That week I had been writing the chapter on fasting in community. I realized how lonely I felt engaging in Friday fasts by myself without the support and encouragement of others. That Friday as I skipped out on fasting I felt like some inner part of myself was affirming that fasting is best in community. It's quite hard to do it alone.

FASTING AND MOURNING

I engaged in another fast while writing this book. It happened quite inadvertently, when my father died. His death was a mercy because he had been ill for quite a while, but I was still deeply affected. Generally I wear a colorful necklace almost every day, but in the first week after his death, I found I was unable to wear jewelry. In the midst of mourning, putting on something brightly colored felt inappropriate.

For a week I simply didn't wear jewelry. Then I decided to wear the plain silver cross I wear during Lent. I wore that cross every day for more than a month after my father's death. I felt as if I were entering into a voluntary Lent, a time of sorrow and self-examination. For many years I have been marking Lent by fasting from the jewelry that normally gives me pleasure, so that particular discipline felt right in the first month after my father died.

As I embraced my out-of-season Lenten discipline after my father's death, I appreciated for the first time the profound relationship between fasting and mourning. When we are deeply sad, the everyday joys of life feel unnatural and inappropriate. Eating, playing music, wearing jewelry, engaging in entertainment, media and so many other everyday pleasures feel awkward and uncomfortable when we are mourning.

Both mourning and fasting are closely connected with longing. After my father died I longed to be free of grief and pain, and I longed for that same freedom for my family members who were mourning with me.

Jesus talks about fasting when the Bridegroom is gone (Mk 2:18-20), and as I mourned my father, I longed for Jesus to come and make all things right. I longed for heaven, where all tears will be wiped away (Rev 21:4).

When we fast, we are affirming that life is best lived in rhythms. On feast days we embrace God's abundant gifts and we rejoice in that abundance. On fast days we mourn and we long for the restoration of all things. Brokenness and abundance coexist in life, and fasting connects us with brokenness even when we are not mourning the death of a loved one. Among our family and friends and in the wider world, we know of sorrow, sadness, ill health, broken relationships and profound need for God.

Fasting connects us with those realities and enables us to engage in mourning for the brokenness of this sad world we live in. Fasting calls us to deepen our intercessory prayer for the needs of people we know and people we don't know. As we fast, we embrace a deep longing for Jesus, who alone can bring wholeness and abundant life. The rhythm of fasting and feasting calls us to embrace both sorrow and gladness in different times and seasons. The Bible is full of both emotions.

Observing the sabbath is another spiritual discipline that affirms the significance of rhythms. Let's compare these two spiritual disciplines— fasting and sabbath keeping—in order to see fasting more clearly.

Like the Sabbath

Sabbath keeping and fasting definitely have some similarities. Both disciplines affirm that rhythms matter. Both disciplines provide a structure for us to set aside one thing for the sake of something else. When we keep the sabbath, we set aside our work and our desire for productivity so we can experience rest in God. When we fast, we stop consuming things like food, entertainment or media so we can pray with more concentration. Both disciplines slow us down and help us reduce our consumption.

The sabbath and fasting address different human needs and compulsions. The sabbath encourages us to face our addiction to being productive, our need to justify ourselves by what we do. As I described in my book *Sabbath Keeping: Finding Freedom in the Rhythms of Rest,* the sabbath teaches grace at a deep and heartfelt place inside us. Because we stop many of our activities on the sabbath, we learn that God loves us apart from what we do.

On the sabbath we embrace abundance. We take the time to notice the abundant life God has given us. We focus on God's gifts, and we engage in prayers of thankfulness. In one Jewish tradition, prayers of intercession are discouraged on the sabbath because even intercession is too much work on a day when we focus on what is rather than what might be. On the sabbath we stop trying to change the world, and we enjoy the world as it is.

Fasting is an invitation to still the noise and listen to the silence, to cut the clutter and see the order, and to slide beneath what is superficial and trivial to that which is worthwhile and lasting.

DAVID TREMBLEY

In Jewish tradition, fasting is forbidden on the sabbath. On the sabbath we feast and rejoice in God's goodness. Keeping the sabbath makes space for God because we stop focusing on what we need to do, what we need to get and what's missing in our lives. The sabbath is a little slice of heaven that we can enjoy one day each week.

In fasting, on the other hand, we embrace emptiness, sacrifice and lack. Fasting reflects the fact that the world is not as it should be, that we are called to pray fervently for the needs of this broken world. When we fast, we engage with the pain of the world, the places where God's abundance hasn't yet reached, the needs of ordinary people that haven't yet been met. Fasting is a step into the heart of God, who grieves for the pain of the people he created and loves.

The sabbath teaches grace, and fasting teaches freedom. When we fast, we are free—briefly—from our needs for food or recreation. We are free to embrace discomfort for a short season. We are free from our need to be strong all the time, our need to control everything and our need to understand everything. Fasting strips away things that are extraneous in order to focus for a season on the thing that really matters, prayer and our relationship with God.

The disciplines of fasting and sabbath keeping are profoundly counter-cultural. The world we live in tells us to be productive and happy every moment. In fact, we often pick up from our culture that something is wrong with us if we aren't busy and optimistic all the time. Sadly, we miss something significant about God if we listen to our culture.

God runs the universe—we do not. We affirm this truth in a special way when we stop working and embrace rest on the sabbath. God cares deeply about the hurting, the lonely, the poor and those who need his love. We affirm this truth in a special way when we fast and pray. We voluntarily set aside our own contentment for a set period of time and embrace discomfort so we can pray for those who live in discomfort. In the midst of our culture's frantic pace and obsession with personal happiness, the rhythms of sabbath keeping and fasting help us step aside from our culture and keep God at the center of our lives.

LEARNING FROM FEASTING AND FASTING

A rhythm of fasting and feasting makes us spiritually healthier. In the same way that fasting lasts for a set time only, so should feasting last only for a time. Our culture tells us to feast all the time, whether it's a feast of food or video games or movies or shopping. To be spiritually healthy, we need to place time limits on our feasting just like we do on our fasting.

If we engage in regular fasts from food, media or shopping, we train ourselves to limit those things in everyday life. We prove to ourselves

Fasting expands our ideas of "feasting" on Christ.

JAN JOHNSON,
FASTING AND SIMPLICITY

that we can live briefly without them, so we are often more able to keep them at healthy levels in daily life. We train ourselves to grasp the profound truth that we don't have to give in to every desire that dances across our minds.

Many people who fast say that they have learned something about feasting on Christ. When we remove the things we normally feast on, we are forced to draw near to God, the giver of every good gift (Jas 1:17), and learn how to experience the feast of goodness that lies in God alone.

TODAY MORE THAN EVER

In the Western world we need fasting today more than ever. Because we are submerged in a sea of advertisements that encourage us to consume endlessly and mindlessly, we need times to withdraw from our consumption to remember what really matters. We need moments of freedom from the forces in our culture that encourage acquisitiveness.

Because the media exposes us to the small number of the super-rich, we forget the very large number of the poor. We eat the foods of affluence and purchase the toys of overconsumption. We need moments of freedom from our obsession with riches so we can remember the poor. More than three hundred passages in the Bible indicate God's concern for the poor, and fasting gives us the freedom to pray for them and experience solidarity with them.

Material poverty is one thing, and spiritual poverty is another. Fasting provides the space and freedom to pray fervently for the spiritual needs of others. Fasting helps us pray that people close to us and people far away would find truth, peace and joy in the gospel of Jesus Christ.

Our world is broken, and we long for the coming of the One who will restore all things and make all things new. We fast to express our longing for the completion and wholeness that Jesus will bring when he returns. We fast to mourn the incomplete and unfulfilled world we live in now. We fast to pray for healing in our broken world, to ask God to bring wholeness, health, life and peace.

Fasting gives us the freedom to feast. If we consume food and possessions and entertainment abundantly each day, we lose the capacity to celebrate. When we fast, we are better able to experience the great joy of feasting. And feasting after a fast nurtures gratitude to God for all his gifts.

Fasting makes space for God by giving us the freedom to set aside our habits for a brief time. Fasting lightens the load by yoking us with Christ in new and unexpected ways. Fasting calls us to pray, enables us to pray and gives power to our prayers in ways we cannot completely understand. Fasting engages us experientially in the mystery of God's love and power. In our day we need fasting more than ever.

QUESTIONS FOR REFLECTION, JOURNALING AND DISCUSSION

1. When you think of freedom in Christ, what comes to mind first? In what ways do you experience freedom in Christ? What kinds of freedom do you long for? Can you see any ways that fasting might contribute to your freedom?

2. Which of your habits have helped you learn that we are called by God to embrace healthy rhythms in our lives? What have those habits taught you? How have they shaped you?

3. What one or two ideas in this book do you think are most important? In what ways do you desire to apply those ideas in your life?

FOR PRAYER

Thank God for what you have learned through healthy habits in your life. Pray about any new spiritual disciplines you would like to embrace. Dedicate your desires and plans to the Lord.

APPENDIX A

FOR FURTHER READING

SOME BOOKS ON FASTING FOR CHRISTIANS

Bright, Bill. *The Transforming Power of Fasting and Prayer: Personal Accounts of Spiritual Renewal.* Orlando: New Life Publications, 1997.

After a brief introduction linking fasting to fulfilling the Great Commission, most of the book consists of testimonies of people who have grown spiritually through fasting from food.

Johnson, Jan. *Simplicity and Fasting.* Downers Grove, Ill.: InterVarsity Press, 2003.

A Bible study guide for groups or individuals on the disciplines of simplicity and fasting, with helpful notes for group leaders.

Piper, John. *A Hunger for God: Desiring God Through Fasting and Prayer.* Wheaton, Ill.: Crossway Books, 1997.

The first part of the book is an excellent discussion of the ways to fast for the right motives: growing in faith and desiring God.

Rogers, Carole Garibaldi. *Fasting: Exploring a Great Spiritual Practice.* Notre Dame, Ind.: Sorin Books, 2004.

The author is a Catholic, and roughly half of the book focuses on Christian fasting. The remainder discusses fasting in other world religions.

Ryan, Thomas. *The Sacred Art of Fasting.* Woodstock, Vt.: Skylight Paths, 2005.

A Catholic priest discusses the Christian tradition of fasting in a clear and helpful way. Approximately half of the book discusses fasting in other religions.

Wallis, Arthur. *God's Chosen Fast.* Fort Washington, Penn.: Christian Literature Crusade, 1986.

A classic book with a wonderful overview of the biblical texts on fasting and a focus on fasting for God's glory rather than for selfish reasons.

HELPFUL CHRISTIAN BOOKS WITH A CHAPTER ON FASTING

Calhoun, Adele Ahlberg. *Spiritual Disciplines Handbook: Practices That Transform Us.* Downers Grove, Ill.: InterVarsity Press, 2005.

A systematic overview of sixty-two spiritual disciplines, with reflection questions and spiritual exercises for each one.

Foster, Richard J. *Celebration of Discipline.* San Francisco: Harper & Row, 1978.

One of the first widely read books with a chapter on fasting.

Jones, Tony. *The Sacred Way: Spiritual Disciplines for Everyday Life.* Grand Rapids: Zondervan, 2005.

A helpful discussion of sixteen spiritual disciplines, with lovely quotations and prayers.

Thompson, Marjorie J. *Soul Feast: An Invitation to the Christian Spiritual Life.* Louisville, Ky.: Westminster John Knox, 1995.

Fasting is set in the context of other spiritual disciplines, with an emphasis on fasting as self-emptying.

Winner, Lauren F. *Mudhouse Sabbath.* Brewster, Mass.: Paraclete, 2003.

Gives a poignant perspective on Christian fasting rooted in Judaism.

A Practical Book on Fasting

Adamson, Eve, and Linda Horning. *The Complete Idiot's Guide to Fasting.* Indianapolis: Alpha Books, 2002.

An excellent source of information about juice and water fasts. The sections on spirituality draw on many religious traditions as well as New Age religion, with only brief mention of fasting in the Christian tradition.

A Few Wonderful Books on Prayer

Foster, Richard J. *Prayer: Finding the Heart's True Home.* San Francisco: HarperSanFrancisco, 1992.

Many people say this book more than any other helped them learn to pray and grow in prayer.

Huggett, Joyce. *The Joy of Listening to God.* Downers Grove, Ill.: InterVarsity Press, 1986.

A practical and biblical explanation of how to hear God in prayer. Huggett helped me learn how to listen to God, and I will always be grateful.

Steindl-Rast, David. *Gratefulness, the Heart of Prayer.* New York: Paulist, 1984.

A terrific exploration of the ways thankfulness in prayer changes our hearts and our lives.

White, John. *Daring to Draw Near: People in Prayer.* Downers Grove, Ill.: InterVarsity Press, 1997.

My all-time favorite book on prayer. It teaches about prayer using examples from the Bible.

Christian Books on Eating Disorders and Body Image

Barger, Lilian Calles. *Eve's Revenge: Women and a Spirituality of the Body.* Grand Rapids: Brazos, 2003.

Barger argues that Jesus is uniquely relevant to the issues many women and some men have with their bodies.

Jantz, Gregory L. *Hope, Help and Healing for Eating Disorders: A New Approach to Treating Anorexia, Bulimia and Overeating.* Colorado Springs: Shaw, 2002.
Addresses the emotional, relational, physical and spiritual dimensions of healing from eating disorders.

Newman, Deborah. *Loving Your Body: Embracing Your True Beauty in Christ.* Colorado Springs: Focus on the Family Publishing, 2002.
Draws on Scripture, research and stories of women who have struggled with negative body image.

SCHOLARLY BOOKS ON TOPICS RELATED TO CHRISTIAN FASTING

Brumberg, Joan Jacobs. *Fasting Girls: The Emergence of Anorexia Nervosa as a Modern Disease.* Cambridge, Mass.: Harvard University Press, 1988.
Discusses fasting among Christian saints and also contains a terrific discussion of the history of dieting in the twentieth century.

Grimm, Veronika E. *From Feasting to Fasting, the Evolution of a Sin.* New York: Routledge, 1996.
Contains a helpful discussion of asceticism in the first Christian centuries.

Shaw, Teresa M. *The Burden of the Flesh: Fasting and Sexuality in Early Christianity.* Minneapolis: Fortress, 1998.
A thought-provoking exploration of fasting and sexuality among Christians in the first four centuries after Christ.

Vandereycken, Walter, and Ron van Deth. *From Fasting Saints to Anorexic Girls: The History of Self-Starvation.* New York: New York University Press, 1994.
The authors describe the extreme fasting habits of female saints throughout church history and compare and contrast them to modern-day anorexics.

APPENDIX B

THE CHALLENGE OF FINDING
FASTING IN THE BIBLE

Four New Testament passages that deal with fasting require a special explanation: Matthew 17:21, Mark 9:29, Acts 10:30 and 1 Corinthians 7:5. In the King James Version of the Bible, which dates from 1610, each of these verses includes the word *fasting,* linking fasting to prayer. Modern translations do not use the word *fasting* in most of these verses. Some of the recent translations put *fasting* in a footnote or in brackets, but in many cases the translations of the past fifty years omit *fasting* in these four passages.

One of the most often quoted New Testament passages on fasting falls into this category. In the Gospel of Mark, when Jesus comes down from the Mount of Transfiguration, he finds his disciples trying very hard to cast an evil spirit out of a boy. They just can't do it. Jesus heals the boy by casting out the evil spirit. Later his disciples ask him why they did not succeed. Jesus replies, "This kind can come out only through prayer" (Mk 9:29 NRSV).

The King James Version of Mark 9:29 reads "prayer and fasting." In many of the newer translations, this verse is footnoted. For example, the New Revised Standard Version's footnote says "Other ancient authorities add *and fasting.*" Matthew 17:21 is an account of the same story. The verse in the King James Version says, "This kind goeth not out but by prayer and fasting."

The King James Version was translated from the Greek texts available in the 1500s, but today there are many more texts to consider. The ancient texts now available date from a much earlier time than the texts available five centuries ago. Scholars generally consider earlier texts to be more likely to reflect the way the Bible was originally written because each time a manuscript was copied by hand, the possibility for changes increased. Those earlier Greek texts do not use the word *fasting* in these verses.

This is counterintuitive. The King James Version, one of the earliest English translations, was based on later Greek texts. The latest English translations, dating from the 1950s onward, are based on earlier Greek texts, which scholars assume to be more accurate because they would have been copied fewer times.

When a later manuscript contains a word that was not in an earlier manuscript, scholars assume that a scribe added that word because he thought it was important. Because the word *fasting* was evidently added to four New Testament passages perhaps two or three centuries after they were first written, we can assume that fasting had a significant place in the Christian practices of the early church. Indeed, in chapter four we looked at fasting in Christian history and saw that the early church did value fasting very highly.

Notes

Chapter 1: An Invitation to Freedom

Page 15:   "The goal of Christian spirituality": Tony Jones, *The Sacred Way: Spiritual Disciplines for Everyday Life* (Grand Rapids: Zondervan, 2005), pp. 26, 29 and 31.

Page 15:   John Piper, author of many books: *A Hunger for God: Desiring God Through Fasting and Prayer* (Wheaton, Ill.: Crossway Books, 1997), pp. 41-42.

Page 16:   Christian fasting is the voluntary denial: This definition is adapted from the definition given by Bruce Wilkinson in *Set Apart: Discovering Personal Victory Through Holiness* (Sisters, Ore.: Multnomah Publishers, 1998), p. 228.

Chapter 2: Food and Fasting Today

Page 21:   Fasting in general was recommended: Teresa M. Shaw, *The Burden of the Flesh: Fasting and Sexuality in Early Christianity* (Minneapolis: Fortress, 1998), p. 9.

Page 22:   "Although fasting and restrictive eating": Joan Jacobs Brumberg, *Fasting Girls: The Emergence of Anorexia Nervosa as a Modern Disease* (Cambridge, Mass.: Harvard University Press, 1988), p. 41.

Page 22   A moderate amount of fat was considered: Ibid., p. 233.

Page 23:   "We are faced with an abundance of food": Ibid., p. 260.

Page 32:   "Hope is the trust": Henri Nouwen, *Bread for the Journey* (San Francisco: HarperSanFrancisco, 1996), in a daily meditation eLetter, January 16, 2006 <www.henrinouwen.org >.

Chapter 3: Motives

Page 45:   Lauren Winner on fasting: Lauren Winner, *Real Sex: The Naked Truth About Chastity* (Grand Rapids: Brazos, 2005), p. 127.

Page 46:   "Fasting is not meant to drag us down": Lauren Winner, *Mudhouse Sabbath* (Brewster, Mass.: Paraclete, 2003), p. 90.

Pages 47-48:   Gerald May points out: Gerald May, *The Awakened Heart,* quoted in *Simpler Living, Compassionate Life: A Christian Perspective,* ed. Mike Schut (Denver: Morehouse, 1999), pp. 45-46.

Chapter 4: A Look at Christian History

Page 52:   "What would account": Richard Foster, *Celebration of Discipline* (San Francisco: Harper & Row, 1988), p. 47.

Pages 53-54:   *The Didache,* an instructional handbook: J. D. Douglas, ed., *The New Interna-tional Dictionary of the Christian Church* (Grand Rapids: Zondervan, 1978), pp. 297-98.

Page 54:   During the third century: Thomas Ryan, *The Sacred Art of Fasting* (Woodstock, Vt.: Skylight Paths Publishing, 2005), pp. 52-53.

Page 54:   Because the persecution of Christians: Walter Vandereycken and Ron Van Deth, *From Fasting Saints to Anorexic Girls* (New York: New York University Press, 1994), p. 21.

Page 55:   "When someone is poor among them": Aristide, quoted in Ryan, *Sacred Art of Fasting,* p. 52.

Page 55:   "In the day on which you fast": *Shepherd of Hermas,* quoted in ibid., p. 46.

Page 55:   Origen blessed those who fasted: Origen, quoted in ibid.

Pages 55-56:   "Break your bread for those who are hungry": Augustine, quoted in ibid., pp. 46-47.

Page 56:   Gregory the Great, bishop of Rome: Gregory the Great, quoted in ibid., p. 48.

Page 56:   "As bodily food fattens the body": John Chrysostom, quoted in Eve Adamson and Linda Horning, *The Complete Idiot's Guide to Fasting* (Indianapolis: Alpha Books, 2002), p. 86.

Page 56:   Earthly desires versus the pure soul: Vandereycken and van Deth, *From Fasting Saints to Anorexic Girls,* p. 18.

Pages 56-57:   "An emaciated body will more readily pass": Tertullian, quoted in ibid., p. 15.

Page 57:   "The stuff of the body": Theresa M. Shaw, *The Burden of the Flesh: Fasting and Sex-uality in Early Christianity* (Minneapolis: Fortress, 1998), p. 3.

Page 57:   "In order to bridle the lusts of the flesh": Carole Garibaldi Rogers, *Fasting: Ex-ploring a Great Spiritual Practice* (Notre Dame, Ind.: Sorin Books, 2004), p. 65.

Page 58:   Bonaventure linked prayer: Bonaventure, quoted in Ryan, *Sacred Art of Fasting,* p. 47.

Page 59   In the late medieval period: Vandereycken and van Deth, *From Fasting Saints to Anorexic Girls,* p. 20.

Page 60:   "One can be damned alone": Quoted in Rogers, *Fasting,* p. 70.

Page 60:   "On fasting I say this": Martin Luther, quoted in John Piper, *A Hunger for God: Desiring God Through Fasting and Praying* (Wheaton, Ill.: Crossway Books, 1997), pp. 185-86.

Page 61:   During the Civil War: Derek Prince, *Shaping History Through Prayer and Fasting* (Springdale, Penn.: Whitaker House, 1973), pp. 185-98.

Page 63:   A number of prominent evangelical Christians: The December 28, 2004, issue of *The Christian Century* had the theme "Turning East: The Appeal of the Ortho-dox Tradition," with three articles about the aspects of the Eastern Orthodox tradition that appeal to Protestants and Catholics.

Pages 64-65:   "To Mother Teresa": Adamson and Horning, *Complete Idiot's Guide to Fasting,* p. 89.

Page 66:   "Some have exalted religious fasting": John Wesley, quoted in Arthur Wallis, *God's Chosen Fast* (Fort Washington, Penn.: Christian Literature Crusade, 1968), p. 74.

Chapter 5: A Photo Album of Biblical Stories

Pages 86-87: "It is as if there is an almost unconscious assumption": Richard Foster, *Celebration of Discipline* (San Francisco: Harper & Row, 1988), p. 52.

Chapter 6: Abstaining from Food

Page 97: To understand what happens: The information about the physiology of fasting from all solid food comes from several books, including Elmer L. Towns, *Fasting for Spiritual Breakthrough* (Ventura, Calif.: Regal, 1996); Elmer L. Towns, *The Beginner's Guide to Fasting* (Ann Arbor, Mich.: Servant, 2001); Ronnie W. Floyd, *The Power of Prayer and Fasting* (Nashville: Broadman & Holman, 1997); James Lee Beall, *The Adventure of Fasting* (Old Tappan, N.J.: Fleming H. Revell, 1974); Stephen Harrod Buhner, *The Fasting Path* (New York: Avery, 2003); Eve Adamson and Linda Horning, *The Complete Idiot's Guide to Fasting* (New York: Alpha Books, 2002); Arthur Wallis, *God's Chosen Fast* (Fort Washington, Penn.: Christian Literature Crusade, 1968); Carole Garibaldi Rogers, *Fasting: Exploring a Great Spiritual Practice* (Notre Dame, Ind.: Sorin Books, 2004); Thomas Ryan, *The Sacred Art of Fasting* (Woodstock, Vt.: Skylight Paths Publishing, 2005); and Joel Furhman, *Fasting—and Eating—for Health* (New York: St. Martin's Griffin, 1995).

Chapter 7: Other Fasts

Page 117: "If you have been brought low": Arthur Wallis, *God's Chosen Fast* (Fort Washington, Penn.: Christian Literature Crusade, 1968), p. 39.

Chapter 9: Today More Than Ever

Page 138: As I described in my book: Lynne Baab, *Sabbath Keeping: Finding Freedom in the Rhythms of Rest* (Downers Grove, Ill.: InterVarsity Press, 2005).

Scripture Index